D1356600

MARY WHITEHOUSE

Mary Whitehouse

by

MAX CAULFIELD

MOWBRAYS
LONDON & OXFORD

© *1975 Max Caulfield*

ISBN 0 264 66190 7

First published 1975
by A. R. Mowbray & Co. Limited,
The Alden Press, Osney Mead,
Oxford OX2 0EG

Printed in Great Britain
by W & J Mackay Limited, Chatham

Contents

CHAPTER ONE

At Home

Speaking in Birmingham on October 19, 1974, Sir Keith Joseph, then considered to be reaching for the leadership of the British Conservative Party, voiced an unexpected eulogy on the honorary general secretary of the National Viewers 'and Listeners' Association (National VALA): 'Let us take inspiration from that admirable woman, Mary Whitehouse,' he exhorted his listeners, a group of Tories still stunned by a second defeat at the polls within nine months. 'We can see in her a shining example of what one person can do single-handedly when inspired by faith and compassion. An unknown, middle-aged woman, a schoolteacher in the Midlands, set out to protect adolescents against the permissiveness of our time. Look at the scale of the opposing forces: the whole of the new establishment, with their sharp words and sneers poised. Today, her name is a household word, made famous by the very assaults on her by her enemies. She has mobilised and given fresh heart to many who see where the current fashion is leading.'

Sir Keith's call for the 'remoralisation of Britain'; for the restoration of 'family and civilised values'; his expressed concern for 'liberties, traditions and morals', all put him squarely within Mrs Whitehouse's camp. Yet he went on to declare, 'I do not accept all her ideas, she will not accept all mine.'

Mary Whitehouse could not dampen down her Christian satisfaction with Sir Keith's call for a remoralisation of what had largely become an amoral society; after all, for years she had been a member of Moral Rearmament, a movement which, whatever you might think of it, was committed to ancient virtues. She had, in fact, risen to national fame with her defence of traditionally held moral values, although many who also held to the tenets of Christian civilisation thought her interpretations often prehistoric. The way was to be paved with tiger traps.

Not that tiger traps, or for that matter, small-bore rifles, 16-inch naval guns, herds of charging elephants, rogue rhinoceroses nor even the thoughts of Chairman Mao can be seen as fairly weighted obstacles or deterrents to that phenomenon—surely unique to the English scene—known as Mary Whitehouse. In one sense, she appears a familiar, almost inevitable figure—the eternal memsahib. Armed with little more than a metaphysical parasol, she has spiritedly engaged the assorted dacoits, headhunters, and bazaar pedlars of the pornography business; in the course of which she has found herself confronting those beavering away in the marxist revolutionary industry. Although there is no rule that a pornographer should be a revolutionary or vice versa, except that they are both anti-establishment, the two seem to have been marching side by side on British television. But let us pause there. Mary Whitehouse insists that she does not believe that she is primarily involved in politics; it is, perhaps, an interesting sidelight that her husband Ernest, a practising Methodist, believes that the Book of Daniel foreshadows the worldwide triumph of Communism (which will, of course, in its turn be subverted, happily, by the disciples of God). For her part, if the agitators belonging to the differing marxist superstitions wish to undermine our western society, she only wishes they would try not to damage the children.

When you push Mary Whitehouse into a corner—which is almost as difficult as ascending the south-west face of Everest—she will scythe the legs from under you with a single, unanswerable argument. By what right do we corrupt innocence?

This is by no means the whole of her argument but it is, almost certainly, the cornerstone.

Mary Whitehouse is ten years younger than this century—which, presumably, puts her at the wrong end of middle-age. Once, I suppose, she would have been considered an *oldish* person but any such view is quickly altered when she ceases to be a disembodied voice on the telephone or an image on the TV screen and materialises in the flesh. Not the least of the astonishing things about a lady who likes to think of herself as a very ordinary person is the way she appears to have cheated degeneration. Were it not for the slightly tell-tale signs of ageing around the throat, her high colouring, trim, unflabby figure and zestful movements would lead you to believe that she was still in her early fifties, an outdoors woman who energetically refereed lacrosse matches or stalked sheep trails in Welsh hills. Neither she nor her husband are all that well-off. She gets paid nothing for her 'work', although she is allowed hotel and travelling expenses where appropriate and keeps all fees earned from writing newspaper articles or from making broadcasting appearances. She manages on a much restricted budget. She is quite likely to greet a visitor at the door of her 140-year-old farmhouse dressed as modishly as is appropriate to her generation; I found her in a bright red trouser-suit at once functional and attractive. If not precisely a dawn person, she is anything but laggard and inclines towards a 6.30 or 7 a.m. rise. The early part of the day is often spent in a stitch-quilted housecoat; a pale, silvery garment which she often gets no opportunity to discard before 11 o'clock. As Mrs Margaret Lawley, her secretary, says, 'Somehow or other, the phone begins to ring almost as soon as she rises, no matter how early she gets up. Often we're right into the day's work before we know where we are and Mrs Whitehouse just doesn't get a chance to get properly dressed. We often laugh when I find her sitting talking to a newspaper editor, TV producer or some important political figure still in her housecoat. I once told her, "It's a good job this isn't on TV—imagine the reports: Mrs Whitehouse only half-dressed!" '

It has not been difficult for those against Mrs Whitehouse and her cause to present her as an almost Grundyish figure who

wears a flowerpot hat and wields an umbrella with all the
ferocity of Giles' grandmother. The idea that Mary Whitehouse
might actually be an extraordinarily normal person seems faintly
preposterous to many. Yet no less a person than Mick Jagger
found that he had got the lady all wrong. When they were
appearing on a TV guest show together, he confided to Mrs
Whitehouse that she wasn't at all what he had imagined her to
be. 'He then said something that really touched me,' declares
Mrs Whitehouse. 'He said he expected me to be the wrong kind
of person and, well, I wasn't at all—and he felt we had a rap-
port.' With the values at present existing in Britain, an endorse-
ment from Mick Jagger might be more prestigious than a life
peerage and Mrs Whitehouse shows every sign of being touched
by his tribute.

Actually Mrs Whitehouse does not type-cast all that easily.
She reveals that she and her husband begin their day with
bible-reading while still abed, but only after having a cup of tea.
Ernest says that he usually gets through three or four chapters a
morning. Before he has finished, Mary has started her secular
task of entering up the previous day's events in her diary before
trotting downstairs to switch on the radio and doing her keep-fit
exercises. She rejoins Ernest for a formal morning prayer after
which they have breakfast of toast, marmalade and fruit (Mary,
according to friends, practically lives on apples) which is preceded by grace as are all meals in the Whitehouse establishment.
It is eaten to the accompaniment of the radio and a swift analysis
of the morning newspapers. After the programme *Today's Papers*,
the BBC is switched off and Mary Whitehouse sets to with con-
tented energy (she may have already answered the telephone at
least a half-dozen times) to cope with the day's post, accepting
or rejecting invitations to address this or that body, or commenting to reporters seeking a controversial quote and so on.
She works chiefly with Mrs Lawley but her husband helps more
now he has retired from business to assist her full time with the
daunting problems confronting the National Viewers' and

Listeners' Association (VALA) which is now seen by many people as an unofficial but influential watchdog of certain British liberties.

The second half of that morning programme seems, surely, hardly distinguishable from the morning routines of such heroes of the left as Hugh Scanlon, Mick McGahey or Arthur Scargill. Yet the shadow of those probably obsolete Christian exercises tends to exude a faint odour of sanctimoniousness. Certainly, those who prefer less Cromwellian lives or ones more relevant to the class struggle might feel put off by them. Nor does her life-style appear to have much connection with those of us who enjoy what has come to be called 'colour-supplement living'. Few could understand what it has to offer those workers who like a booze up in the Sunderland Boilermakers' Union club or those who, having emerged from an upper working class or lower middle-class upbringing within the last twenty years to enjoy the butterfly existence of an 'executive', are now only satisfied with double-garages, company Jaguars and wife-swapping parties.

Life at Triangle Farm House, Far Forest, near Kidderminster, Worcestershire, fails to fall neatly into a slot which would enable one to be snide. An acre of ground surrounds the house. Most of this is fairly rough-looking and when Mrs Whitehouse labels it 'meadow' it seems rather euphemistic. Anyway the acre doesn't look all that middle-class and, if not exactly Merseyside waste-land, I suspect that most British manual workers, living in their neat, flower-fringed semi-detatched houses, would certainly turn their noses up at it. The summerhouse at the bottom of the garden suggests Edwardian opulence but the mirage quickly dissolves when you approach it—in winter at least—for it often turns into a muddy track. Though the setting is very beautiful, you search in vain for a well kept lawn. Mrs Whitehouse, one learns, paid for the summerhouse by writing books and newspaper articles. In fact it strikes rather a Fabian note: One is reminded that Bernard Shaw did all his work in a hut at the bottom of his garden. Mrs Whitehouse works here throughout the warmer months, linked to the outside world by a telephone extension.

Mrs Whitehouse, of course, enjoys a view over an area of protected natural beauty called the Wyre Forest with the Clee Hills in mid-distance. She has described this view to a Fleet Street woman reporter called Maureen Cleave as '*most* beautiful' —the lady expertly catching the fact that Mrs Whitehouse tends to emphasise certain words to clarify her opinions. Did she ever walk in this pleasant forest? Mrs Whitehouse's startled reply was a hearty, 'Oh, golly, no! I never get so far as going into the forest.' The best she could do, it appeared, was walk for at least twenty-five minutes each day through the quiet countryside with its kingfishers and honeysuckle. She told Miss Cleave, 'When I walk in these lanes, all my tensions fall away. If I am searching for an inspired way to do something, being in the countryside is like being in a cathedral to me.'

Surprisingly Mrs Whitehouse does not attend church every Sunday these days although she still considers herself a faithful Anglican. 'I find I get my spiritual food from the countryside,' she explained. When Miss Cleave observed how healthy she looked she drew yet another astonishing counter: 'It's funny that you should say I look healthy because I used not to be. I have no doubt that I have been given a new source of health and strength.' Maureen Cleave, perhaps the first Fleet Street voice to suggest that Mrs Whitehouse was a serious figure, could not help but add, 'Where Mrs Whitehouse scores over most of her adversaries is in the certain knowledge that God is on her side.'

Mrs Whitehouse finds little time to read books outside her subject, but she has a well-developed sense of history and of the struggle of man towards civilisation. The school where she last taught is only a mile or so from Ironbridge, a birthplace of the Industrial Revolution (among her most cherished mementoes are samples of Coalport china, fished up from the river Severn where some pieces have lain since the eighteenth century and which have now become prized objects). With me, she also displayed her pride and pleasure in the great forest about her and its history; she pointed out that trees from the Wyre Forest were cut down to provide the charcoal which first smelted iron. And only a few hundred yards away stood Furnace Mill, once occupied by the Roundheads before their attack on Bridgnorth —and again the trees of the forest had been used: this time to smelt Sectarian cannonballs.

Mrs Whitehouse's acre, despite its historic associations and generally countrified surroundings, sits in a relatively crowded area of cottages and spruced-up houses which lend it a vague air of semi-suburbia; however, it carries its quota of hens, geese and fantail pigeons, plus a sandpile in the large space at the rear of the house where Mary's grandchildren can play. The space is also used for the cars run by Mary and Ernest (the Association allows her a small runabout). The garage is a wooden structure, very farmish. Throughout the keynote is simplicity without any suburban ultra-neatness.

The house itself is also non-pretentious though very comfortable. It has been converted and a relatively large lounge on the ground floor with the Whitehouse main bedroom above it has been added. There is also a dining room, a spacious hall, three other fair-sized bedrooms and a cosy ground-floor room with an open grate where logs are burned, which has been christened 'the snug.' This room houses a second (colour) TV set and also has a phone extension. It is, therefore, the room where the Whitehouses do most of their viewing, most of their living and a great deal of their work. The house is completed by a long, modernised kitchen, at the end of which lies the square 'office' with its filing cabinets, typewriters and desks where Mrs Lawley spends most of her day. The decor throughout is informal—lived-in and liveable-in, in no particular style. Passing through the house, one notices that Mrs Whitehouse collects rare rocks and pebbles which lie piled up in careless confusion on the shelf under a window.

It is scarcely remarkable that the Whitehouses lead a simple life. When the sixties are reached, you tend to cut out some of the frills, anyway; but, in addition, in their case, the Whitehouses have dedicated themselves to Mary's work even to the extent of financial disadvantage. They rarely entertain, eat sparingly but nourishingly mainly on the produce from their garden and fresh brown eggs from their hens and they still have much of the furniture they bought when they were first married. Yet the idea that this might be a puritanical or even ascetic household is untrue. The Whitehouses are easy-going, notably unstarchy, the souls of hospitality and warmth. Together they provide good company if you enjoy intelligent conversation—if only on a restricted range of topics—and a quiet but affable wit. For a couple who have found themselves under attack as the quintessence of intolerance, they seemed to me—and I can only speak as I found them—surprisingly open-minded. Much of their conversation is inevitably 'shoptalk': God, the Bible, the morals of the age, the return of hedonism and paganism after two thousand years of civilisation. It is shop talk of course on an elevated plane —and socially permissible in that it is what they are primarily concerned with in their lives. Objectively, they are not any more obsessional than a Fleet Street journalist and their obsession is perhaps less deplorable in that it offers penetrating thoughtfulness.

Ernest Whitehouse is a silver-haired, soft-spoken man who, like his wife, shows an astonishing youthfulness. Well-scrubbed in appearance, he is mildly self-effacing but possesses much quiet strength and non-demonstrative determination. The word 'sex' bothers him not at all. With the precise detachment of a surgeon, he lays much of the blame for the Christian church's alleged anti-sex attitudes on St Paul—or, at least, on the popular interpretations of what St Paul said.

On the whole, the Whitehouses contradict most of the popular misconceptions about them. Neither really flaunts the Bible as the old-fashioned bible-thumpers of my youth did. The greatest of the misconceptions, possibly—that Mary Whitehouse

in herself is some sort of puritanical, anti-fun, anti-sex character
—rapidly dissolves also.

A television crew once spent two or three days in the Whitehouse home making a programme about her; she remembers
their kindness, good-humour and informality ('they would tell
me to put my legs up on the sofa while they marched off to the
kitchen and prepared eggs and bacon') but nonetheless they
were so conditioned by their preconceptions that they found
their normal subject and style of conversation, well-larded with
lewd and vulgar language, so inhibited that they apparently
never so much as once employed a swear-word; the result was
they were no sooner clear of Triangle Farm than they opened
wide the windows of their car and hurled obscenity after obscenity into the air, to relieve their pent-up feelings. They need not,
I think, have really worried.

Mary Whitehouse thus easily confounds many of the preconceptions people may have of her. She is, first of all, quite good
company; she has what Anthony Smith, former editor of the
BBC TV programme *24 Hours*, calls 'star quality'—that is, she
gives off an indefinable luminosity; that strange quality we call
'personality'. It is a word that has been much abused. Very
ordinary, indeed, apparently nondescript people like the TV
interviewer Michael Parkinson often earn the soubriquet for no
better reason than that they have the nerve to parade their
personal and intellectual deficiencies in public without any sense
of misgiving. Yet restricted to its true sense—a genuine magnet-
ism that owes nothing to constant exposure to publicity—it is a
rare enough quality; and Mary Whitehouse appears to have it.
To be quite fair to her, she would be astonished at any suggestion
that she is a 'star'; what she has got is a clear conception of her
duty.

She is, as Maureen Cleave noted, 'a ready laugher'. She
roared with merriment at Jonathan Miller's description of her
anger as 'paranoic'; describes one of her most learned opponents
as 'a bit of a monkey'. The labels that have been stuck on her,

all tend, I discovered, to have been put on the wrong person; as though a vintner's assistant had stuck a Sandeman's Port label on a bottle of Speyside malt.

Yet, in a sense, it is easy enough to understand the attitude of the TV crew who, faced with a jolly, seemingly uncomplicated, obviously normal type of housewife, nevertheless believed that her strictures on BBC behaviour indicated a puritanism on a par with the Victorian ladies who found something smutty about uncovered piano legs. One does, to be frank, enter her home as though it held some of the sanctity of the cloister; yet one rapidly realises that the effect has been produced by having been previously brainwashed. I am not suggesting that Mary or her husband would welcome guests who loosed streams of oaths but they are as mature and, so far as I could judge, as well-balanced as most people.

William Deedes, the journalist and former Conservative MP, has a story which illustrates the dispassionate nature of Mary Whitehouse's methods. 'She asked me if I would go and have dinner with her—and bring along a colleague. She had one of the Danish policemen over—and we all sat down to dinner. Right away, she began urging him to tell us what he dealt with —it was with vice and pornography. Rather shyly, he started to tell us. But none of it was very shocking and very determinedly she urged him again, "Yes, yes, but tell them about such and such". At this stage, the poor man hadn't even got down to his soup—but she forced him to loosen up and tell us about some of the more unattractive sides of Danish porn. What struck me— and particularly my colleague who was totally covered in confusion—was the absolute insouciance with which she insisted that this man trotted out his stuff. For all her considerable degree of sensitivity, she's totally businesslike. She's dedicated—behaving like a lawyer with a brief as she leafs over publications which are really quite disagreeable. "Now what do you think of this? What about that?" I don't think I've ever met a woman who showed me examples of pornography with such aplomb. It is an important part of her gift. But it comes to the stranger as a surprise. However, when she is showing you this stuff, she is behaving no differently from a woman doctor examining you anatomically.'

She is no longer, therefore, if she ever were, a mawkish or easily embarrassed person.

CHAPTER TWO

The Start of it All

As time passes, so the influence and voice of Mary Whitehouse spreads farther and is heard with increasing frequency throughout the country. As I write, it is only a few days since she appeared on a BBC 2 programme, chaired by David Frost, and battled with Mrs Hermin Whitfield of *Grapevine*, a voluntary group seeking to encourage promiscuous girls of West Indian origin to use birth control methods rather than conceive illegitimate children. 'Why doesn't somebody try to educate them to use self-control?' demanded Mrs Whitehouse exasperatedly. She has since castigated the BBC for demanding an increase in the licence fee while spending £300,000 to make a series based on that vaguely ribald classic, the *Memoirs of Casanova*; £150,000 to make what many saw as a rabble-rousing documentary-play, *Leeds United*; a 'fantastic sum'—or so it was alleged—to hire an airfield to light up the name of pop singer Shirley Bassey; and unguesstimable sums, or so it was also alleged, to send, as a more or less regular routine, two or more news camera teams to 'cover' the same news story. The 1974 Christmas issue of the *Listener*, a BBC magazine, featured her name on its front page and allowed her to nominate some of the programmes of which she had approved during the year. Many of the criticisms levelled at her have been on the basis that if she were permitted to 'censor' television programmes, the results would be a series of bland, gutless wonders that would make the output of American TV seem the product of some Augustan age. In this instance, her choice included *The Pallisers* (loosely based on Trollope), two ITV programmes, *South Riding* and *Upstairs Downstairs* (some episodes of which dealt with the Great War) and a piece of light 'entertainment' called *The Generation Game*. If scarcely inspiring, the material seemed neither more nor less edifying than *Play for Today*. On the other hand, none of her choices was likely to inflame a mob to revolution, hasten the decay of capitalism or promote a wider appreciation of full-frontal nudity.

It is, perhaps, typical of Mrs Whitehouse's present modes of attack that none of her offensives appear entirely irrational; however Balaclavan her original forays into the area of public discussion were ten years or so ago, today she uses her arguments with all the skill of a Wellington deploying guerilla troops in the Peninsula.

Mary Whitehouse's critics, of course, rarely hesitate to use their power or influence, including access to a national newspaper, to denigrate her. Yet whatever the faults and misdemeanours they affect to see in her, they rarely make out a case against her. For example, a *Guardian* reporter, Peter Fiddick, had scarcely read his issue of the *Listener* than he sat down to parody her opinions. Fiddick was specifically upset, it seems, that Mrs Whitehouse should attack the BBC over Casanova. Why, he asked astonishingly, did she not attack Sir Lew Grade, head of ATV, who had announced that he was spending *ten million dollars* on a life of Christ? Sir Lew, after all, was not asking licence payers for more money, nor, even by the standards of TV commentators, could you pretend that there was no substantial difference in degree between the lives of Christ and Casanova. Fiddick went on to claim Mrs Whitehouse's long and well-publicised campaign essentially was about over-expenditure whereas her real complaint is that the BBC might not need to raise more money if it cut out the smut, violence, perversion and subversion which, she believes, have characterised the Corporation's output over a long period. Mrs Whitehouse and her cause, naturally, have thrived in the face of such ill-considered and rambling sophistries and her arguments, by contrast, have a refreshing cogency.

Mary Whitehouse was earning £1,500 a year (with pension rights) as Senior Mistress, with responsibility for Art, at Madeley Secondary School, Shropshire. At one stage of her life she actually lived only a few doors from Enoch Powell. At the beginning of 1963, she abruptly became aware that the BBC had—as it appeared to her—ceased to be the impeccable Reithian institution which had once earned the admiration of the world. For almost a half-century, she thought, BBC Radio and television services had been among the most powerful forces for popular education ever devised. For millions of children born in what were once educationally deprived homes, it provided a new world of genius and intelligence and beauty. All those particular pleasures which had, hitherto, been the prerogative of only the rich and leisured classes had been made available to those who wanted to listen. It had all been a rather noble and astonishing achievement. During the war, the Corporation had shown amazing resilience, resisting an almost imperative need to become merely a propaganda instrument. If only because it had relayed Churchill's own words to the inhabitants of the island at a moment of crisis, it had played a key role in assisting to put paid to one particular form of tyranny.

By the standards of the Nineteen Seventies, 1963 does not, in retrospect, appear all that significant. Yet Mary Whitehouse sees it as 'an extraordinary year, a climactic year, the year of the Profumo scandal, *Honest to God*, "kitchen sink" plays, late night satire; the year in which Dr Peter Henderson, Principal Medical Officer of the Ministry of Education, announced that "It was not unchaste" to have pre-marital sex, Dr Alex Comfort defined (on television) a chivalrous boy "as one who takes contraceptives with him when he goes to meet his girl-friend" and the BBC gave the "full treatment" to the exponents of the New Morality and censored, by exclusion, the protagonists of established morality.' Probably on reflection Mary Whitehouse would agree that these items hardly sit four-square; Profumo's romp, for example, could hardly have much causal link with late night satire except to feed it with material.

Up until that year, give and take the rub of life, Mary White-house had been quietly enjoying herself. Children brought up in a drab English provincial town, the offspring of homes that had been rarely exposed to any enlightenment, turned up daily to her art classes with 'little bags and boxes full of samples of bark, sand and tea, paper and cloth, lentils and sugar, candles and cotton wool, "glitter" and leaves'. From such primitive materials, they produced 'exciting, gay and even elegant compositions'. In the summer, she took her students on rambles into the country-side, watched them revel in nature, encouraged children who had never been in an art gallery or, perhaps, even knew what one was, to draw, paint and sculpt. However one regards her subsequent activities, she appears to have found herself admir-ably occupied.

Art, however, was not her only pre-occupation. As Senior Mistress, she had major responsibility for the health and welfare of the girls—and this, by an accident of timing, led her into the business of sex education among the young. Shortly before she joined the school, marriage guidance counsellors had been invited by the headmaster at Madeley to give sex lessons, com-plete with film strips, to fourth-year students. Mary Whitehouse admits that she had reservations about the value of such instruc-tion in schools. It was not really a question of distaste for the subject—she and her husband had practised frankness and 'openness' on the matter in their own home with their three young sons. But it seemed one thing to answer questions naturally and nonchalantly and to put sex and its consequences into their proper context and another to submit the sensitivities of children to possibly violent assault.

Although impressed by the sincerity of the visiting doctor, neither Mrs Whitehouse nor the rest of the staff were any too happy at the counsellor's demand that the staff should be ex-cluded during the lessons. In the end a compromise was reached, with the staff allowed to circle about as unobtrusively as possible.

The teachers' main contribution was to distribute a questionnaire after each lesson. Mary admits that a large number of boys and girls unquestionably benefited from the instruction but she points out that, as always, there were those whose natures refused to conform. One child actually fell off her chair in a faint. Mary also felt that in some cases the instruction drove a wedge between parents, the natural informants, and child: one boy admitted that having learned all the 'facts' from the counsellor, he no longer felt any need to consult his father.

It was this sort of thing that, in a sense, highlighted the one crucial element missing from the series of talks—this and such queries as one from a young girl who asked as an afterthought 'What do you do when a boy wants to go too far?' The series contained no moral element, although the Newsom Report on Secondary Education (1963) had stressed that sex education had to be given on the basis of 'chastity before marriage and fidelity within it'. When the first series of talks was finished, the staff decided the counsellors were no longer needed and that sex education should be handled as only one of a number of subjects linked together and called 'Education for Living'; an essential element here was that the parents were to be given the opportunity of attending and discovering for themselves exactly what it was that their children were being taught. The implications of the change were that the youngsters might also be taught something of the moral concepts involved in sex.

It has been a relatively easy business for those who want a more 'open' society—one, it might be argued, where liberty is allowed to degenerate into licence—to smear Mrs Whitehouse as a narrow-minded puritan. This has been done by ignoring her work in the field of sex education among the young. She claims that the youngsters in this Shropshire Secondary School who were hardly the products of 'middle-class' homes 'approached maturity with a touching idealism and high standards'. She became convinced, as a result of her conversations with them, dealing with questions relating to home, marriage,

family and so on, that if they could be left to their own inclina-
tions, they would not 'walk the road mapped out for them by the
libertarians of our permissive society'. She saw a generation of
youngsters exposed to a new form of insecurity—no longer the
economic one that had been the plague of previous centuries but
that of lack of moral guidance; through a failure within the
Established English church and of English society in itself, they
were left without any yardstick of behaviour by which they
could judge the world around them. She saw them suddenly, not
as the offspring of a liberated and enlightened society but of one
teetering on the brink of chaos, innocent targets for every kind of
commercial and emotional exploitation. She and her colleagues,
in fact, discerned in the 'pop culture' of those early 1960s a
sinister force. In a series of social studies, the children were
taught to recognise that behind the brassy, rowdy and at times
hysterically violent eruption of sound lay something far from
just an innocent, if ear-splitting noise. The 'underground', with
its 'drug scene' and sexual excess, was separated and identified
as the root of much of this 'culture' and the political and pornographic nature of much of its output was exposed. As to the
purpose of all this frenzy—it was easy to explain that the forces
of revolution, unable to achieve their objectives at the ballot box
or, because of the existence of the nuclear bomb, by full-scale
war, were endeavouring to encourage moral decay.

By the very nature of these studies, Mary Whitehouse herself
began to see even more clearly the kind of society in which
modern youngsters found themselves. She had always thought of
herself—and her husband—as conservatives with a small 'c';
that is, she accepted that the world was a far from perfect place
but believed that with thought, effort and goodwill, the lot of
men could be improved. The basis for this improvement, she
believed, lay in the words of Christ—had he not taught that all
men were brothers and that you should love your neighbour as
yourself?

Politics she saw as only a part of a greater sphere and she felt no doctrinaire attachment to any of the differing British political parties; she usually voted Conservative but when she thought their policies inappropriate, she voted Labour, despite its roots in Marxism. She tended to see herself, as most English persons do, as liberal or social democratic. If she jostled on occasions with those on the political fringes as for instance with Enoch Powell, it was because the man himself had a strident voice which some would listen to or because, by chance, he happened to be on her side on some issue and could help her cause. She was very definitely *not* a Powellite.

But her real concerns were children and what the adult world was seeking to do to them. She wrote: 'To draw a battle line is often costly but the rewards in increased respect and honest communication are immense. Children are not fools and nothing is gained by talking down to them. They get mad if we switch off in the middle of a sexy or sadistic television play out of our own prejudices, but if we give them the facts—that plays of this kind can sap energy, tire with fear and feed with false values, they respond to being treated as responsible adults.

'We can help children to become aware of the pressures of advertising. Sex sells, and women are sold cheaper than anything. The theme of a so-called successful sex life is constantly reiterated in one way or another, but much of this can be debunked—and thereby defused—when motives and techniques are understood. It is surely difficult to doubt that the use of women as advertising props has played its part in lowering the status of motherhood, family and home.'

Yet it was an uphill fight where ultimate victory could never really be reached. In the early part of that year, 1963, three girls and two boys stood before her; they had been, according to other children in the class, 'doing things they shouldn't'.

'Why?' she demanded of them.

'Well, miss' replied the spokesman, 'We watched them talking about girls on TV and it looked as it was easy and see how well they done out of it, miss, so we thought we'd try.'

Television was already something of a *bête noir* so far as Mary Whitehouse was concerned. She had spent much time trying to instil into the girls in her care a reverence for and an understanding of the mysteries and mystiques of motherhood. But a single episode of an American soap-opera called *Dr Kildare* dealing with childbirth with good camera work and sound recording but making the most of the 'mother's' screams had, she discovered, terrified a group of girls who told her they were determined never to have babies themselves. Although she realised that the effects were unlikely to be permanent, Mrs Whitehouse saw more clearly than ever that TV could not only be used to manipulate the minds of people—both young and old alike—but in the hands of insensitive and unimaginative fools, could do considerable, if unintentional, damage.

The flashpoint was a *Meeting Point* programme broadcast on March 8, 1963. Of this, Paul Johnson, journalist and former editor of the *New Statesman* wrote: 'Amazing the advice young people get nowadays. I switched on BBC television to hear a panel of experts talking about pre-marital sex. They consisted of a psychologist, a bishop's wife, a headmistress and a clergyman. Although none of them dared to say it outright, they all seemed in favour of sex before marriage if certain conditions were fulfilled. Nobody was prepared to take the orthodox line of traditional Christian morals. The clergyman was twice pressed to say whether or not fornication was a sin, but declined to give any direct answer.'

Mrs Whitehouse herself did not see the programme. But she soon learned of it. As she walked into school the following morning, a small group of fourth-year girls met her at the gate and in some excitement asked her if she had seen the programme the previous evening—'it was about pre-marital sex' and 'ever so interesting'. At social studies later that morning, one of the girls announced, 'I know what's right now, miss.'

'Good, well you tell us,' suggested Mrs Whitehouse.

'Well, I know now that I mustn't have intercourse until I'm engaged.'

In the current atmosphere in Britain, it is relatively easy to damn anybody who makes a fetish out of sex. Many of the old ethical sanctions no longer appear to have any rational basis. When the sex act almost inevitably led to procreation, an entire legal and moral code was necessary to protect mother and child; when the natural consequences of copulation can be artificially avoided it is, perhaps, an entirely new game. When Christ spoke out against the fornicator, the evils of such conduct were clear-cut. The fornicator in essence stole another man's woman—as much a thief as if he had snatched his purse; he also saddled the woman with an unwanted child and left both to the mercies of providence; fornication, therefore, was a criminal offence. Nor, it can be argued, is it much less than criminal now. Men are robbed of potential unsullied partners; children are born illegitimately and left to the mercies of the state or to the woman's ability to fend for herself and her child in a harsh economic world. So it is not merely, as Rabelais used to say, 'a question of the rubbing of the bacon together'—a chemical effusion which provides quite legitimate pleasures. It is not the sex act—but its consequences that can be so dire. And, it would be argued by Mary Whitehouse and others who think like her, that the existing legal and moral code ought not to be supplanted until some better and equally just sanction can be devised.

Yet as our culture moved on; as science opened up new avenues of possible philosophical and metaphysical thought and behaviour; as our society, hard-pressed by affluence and the phenomenon of rising expectations on the one hand and the threat of sudden extinction on the other, needed a whole series of new safety valves, it became possible to argue in favour of another look at the codes which bound sexual conduct. Yet there seemed to be no case for the increasing exploitation of women through advertising, sex magazines, nude pictures and blue movies. The assault on this front came not from men and women of truly liberated minds, concerned with improving mankind, but from vicious little people who recognised a commercial product when they saw one. Sex became an all-pervasive product—everybody began selling it. The 'consumers', far from reaching a state of nirvana, or that deep tranquillity and contentment that the proper experience of sex can bring, often found themselves driven to a state of frenzy induced by titillation piled on titillation. Those who had managed to sate or blunt the normal sexual appetite sought new methods of arousing themselves by perversion so that, as *Le Monde* reported from Paris, a young woman managed to make a name and a fortune for herself by performing the sex act with stallions, dogs and other animals for the benefit of *voyeurs*. Those who argued that the lid should be kept on the pot—if not exactly screwed down tight—found themselves legitimately pointing to the fact that sado-masochistic practices were on the increase. Obviously sadism and masochism themselves were as old as the human race itself; it was the promotion of these as a 'norm' that worried people like Mrs Whitehouse. The whole purpose of Christian moral teaching was to instil a respect and reverence by one man for another. Violence was not a way of life to which she could subscribe—nor did she think it a way of life that would appeal to society as a whole. For every sadist who found happiness in inflicting pain or death on people, there was at least one victim who had to suffer.

Violence on television, therefore, as well as sex, worried Mrs Whitehouse. During a discussion in class on family relations, one shy diffident girl revealed that she had been dreadfully frightened by a film shown in the International Film series on BBC. This showed a young boy and girl watching two men assault a young woman who had run out of a fairground into a field. The sight of this assault aroused the desire of the young man who turned and eyed his companion in a new way, thus causing the girl to flee from him. The shy student admitted to Mrs Whitehouse, 'That made me think what boys might do to me, miss, and ever since I've been so afraid of them that I won't even sit alone in the room with my own brother.'

It is easy to charge Mrs Whitehouse with having been obsessed with sex; difficult, even impossible, for her to plausibly controvert the charge. She was, after all, deeply involved in teaching and guiding young persons on the threshold of puberty. She had to listen to a group of girls admit that as the 'smart and successful' people portrayed on TV seemed to thrive on promiscuity they, too, felt it was the right thing to do; heard some also admit that they took sexy ideas imbibed from TV plays to bed with them and then relived the experience, substituting themselves and either their boy-friend or some pop-idol. Much of this could be easily—and perhaps rightly—dismissed by those who wanted to argue that a television service intended to appeal to a whole spectrum of intellects and tastes could hardly be based on the extreme reactions of a single shy, diffident child; nor could it be seriously proposed that television was responsible for adolescent day and night-dreams. Yet up in her Midland and provincial fastness, Mrs Whitehouse was entitled to feel that the 'smart sophisticates' who lived in their own strange world of electronics and jostling personalities, burgeoning egos and bruised vanities—in short, those who controlled or ran BBC TV —were really closeted in an ivory tower. There were knaves there, obviously, but also fools. Thick-skinned professionals who had lost all claim to sensitivity; foxy little men burrowing away with their sinister plans for a sovietised Britain; 'liberals' who really had no idea what it was all about but would make their grandmothers go-go girls if that became the 'trendy' thing to do.

In a sense, everything depended on who you were and the position where you were standing.

The end came for Mrs Whitehouse when the mother of one of her students came to her in distress to tell her that the girl had 'gone off with a boy' a couple of nights earlier. Apparently the mother had managed to keep the girl well under control until that evening. 'But I can't stop her watching television, can I?' said the distressed mother.

'But why should you?' demanded Mrs Whitehouse.

'Well, she was sitting right in front of the TV screen watching one of those plays and when it got to the sexy part I could see her getting redder and redder in the face, she was so worked up. Then she got up and ran straight out of the house and went off with this boy.'

Dr Alex Comfort's remarks on the BBC TV programme, *This Nation Tomorrow* of July 14, 1963, had also had unfortunate results. Spurred by Dr Comfort's words that a chivalrous boy was one 'who takes contraceptives with him when he goes to meet his girl friend', a 16-year-old boy put this advice into practice—only to turn up a few weeks later at a VD clinic run by a doctor friend of Mrs Whitehouse suffering from gonorrhoea.

None of it, of course, quite hangs together. The girl who had 'gone off' with the boy was, as Mrs Whitehouse has admitted, always 'after' boys, anyway. Boys, too, have been catching gonorrhoea for centuries without the benefit of Dr Comfort's injunction. However, on the other hand, some people may well ask: would the lad's action have been morally defensible if he had *not* caught gonorrhoea? Yet although the examples of damage done do not by themselves prove that damage had been caused by television, one or two things *were* beyond dispute. Children could be easily frightened or titillated by some of the material they saw on TV. And such was the compulsive power of 'the box' that obviously right through society there would be those suffering from mental or emotional deficiencies who might also be disturbed. It was easy for the TV moguls to argue that they could not hope to insulate helpless minorities against the facts of life; yet there was an older wisdom still around which taught that the best way to avoid trouble was to avoid temptation. Places, situations and personal contacts which could not fail but to lead someone into trouble could be avoided.

Mary Whitehouse had, therefore, become aware, as had

many other English Christians, that a host bearing the flamboyant banners of anti-Christian values was now on the march through England. That *Meeting Point* had shocked her. The subject, *What Kind of Loving?*, she readily admitted was an eminently debatable one. In retrospect it would appear a classic turning point to her, not only for the message it had succeeded in putting across to unformed minds but rather more because none of the panel had tried to defend the traditional Christian standpoint; had dared to be anything but trendy. Then there was Bishop Robinson whose *Honest to God* challenged such concepts as the Resurrection and other basic fundamentals. Analysing the BBC's output, Mary Whitehouse considered she discerned an alarming bias; the new writers being encouraged by the Corporation were, seemingly to a man, of the revolutionary Left at its most licentious and anarchic, eager to ridicule and undermine the Christian culture; in debates on religion or morality, humanists, and upholders of 'South Bank' theology were allowed a voice out of all proportion to their numbers.

On the whole, most of the country's inhabitants tend to take what they are given by the BBC and ITA. Attempts to lodge serious complaints generally lead to an experience akin to banging one's fist into a sponge: a piping female voice promises to pass on the complaint—and the caller realises that he has been wasting his breath. Private objections are invariably mislaid in the great maw of the Corporation's bureaucracy; unless, that is, as Mary Whitehouse herself initially discovered, one does not just simply get the brush-off. Almost the first time she telephoned the BBC, for example, the Duty Officer advised her to switch off if she did not like what was being shown. It was a piece of megalomania that aroused the ire of Harmon Grisewood, at that time Chief Assistant to the Director-General, when Mary Whitehouse told him about it—'we don't run the Corporation on the basis that people can switch off' he commented angrily.

During the school holidays of 1963, Mary Whitehouse finally

decided to do something about it all. She decided—in effect—
to take on the massed might of the British Broadcasting Corporation. Perhaps, to be more accurate, the intention was rather less
grandiose than that; no more than a simple move to draw the
attention of reasonable men and responsible authorities to
certain facts. She would confront both the BBC and the ITA
(now IBA) with evidence as to the harmful effects of some TV
output on the minds and emotions of pubescent youngsters.

She requested an interview with Sir Hugh Greene, BBC
Director-General, a genial giant who had been a foreign correspondent on the European mainland before the war and
who had helped organise and run British propaganda services
during the war; a man whose other claim to fame at the beginning of the sixties was probably, that he was the brother of
Graham Greene, the novelist. Grisewood replied that Greene
was out of the country and would not be back for several weeks;
did she wish to postpone her visit to Broadcasting House or
would she care to talk to him?

On the whole, it was rather an extraordinary response—for
who, after all, had ever heard of Mary Whitehouse and exactly
why should she be given direct access to the second most powerful man in the BBC hierarchy? Senior Mistresses at Midland
secondary schools do not, on the whole, stir the juices of the men
who run television the way politicians do. Mary Whitehouse,
however, was not the person to take into account such considera-
tions or to let the grass grow under her feet. She readily admits
that sheer naivety was probably one of the strongest weapons in
her armoury. Besides she would be back at school before Greene
returned from abroad; so she elected to see Harmon Grisewood.
Brother to Freddie, the well-known radio question master,
Grisewood treated her, as she happily admits, with the utmost
courtesy and consideration. He was clearly a man who belonged
to the old Reithian school; and she was in no way surprised
when he resigned from the BBC shortly afterwards. At their
interview, she got the impression that he, too, was concerned

about current trends within the BBC although, after listening to her accounts of the effect of the notorious *Meeting Point* programme on her students, he was sufficiently worldly and alert to the times to ask her if it were not really true that most young people nowadays accepted pre-marital sex as normal. Mrs Whitehouse reassured him: 'No I don't think so—certainly not among the young people I know' and suggested he should meet some of them. He and his wife, to her delight, agreed to have supper with them and a meeting was arranged in a small London flat where the Chief Assistant met 14-year-old Pauline, her friend Anne, young Richard Whitehouse, then studying at the Birmingham College of Art, an Oxford Rhodes Scholar and other youngsters. Not, it might be argued, a definitive cross-section of British young, yet at least an articulate group who declared, as Mrs Whitehouse puts it, 'that the standards of swinging London were not theirs'.

In those summer weeks—for those who wonder how a national phenomenon gets itself going in the first place—Mary Whitehouse also went to see her local MP (Jasper More, MP for Ludlow who was to stand by her side in the years ahead); Dr Mark Hodson, Bishop of Hereford, who became a close friend and adviser; and the then relatively quiescent MP for Wolverhampton and Minister of Health, a certain Mr Powell.

With the feeling that she had done her bit to put things to rights, Mary Whitehouse returned to her task at Madeley, convinced—as she now admits in a 'ridiculously naive way'—that changes would be made. Now that that great institution, the BBC, had been alerted to the errors of its ways, surely it would take note of the feelings that undoubtedly existed in the country.

Instead—and to quote her directly again—the BBC (already under fire from several quarters for its pseudo-satirical late night show, *That Was The Week That Was*) that autumn reached 'a level of depravity not seen before or—with some notable exceptions—since.'

Something more than a few quiet and pleasant chats, it

seemed, would be needed before the great juggernaut that was the BBC could be brought to the point where it neither would nor could choose to ignore what might be called the seventy-mile-an-hour speed limit.

CHAPTER THREE

Mary's Early Life and Marriage

Mary Whitehouse was born Mary Hutcheson, daughter of a Scot. If not of distinguished lineage, the Hutchesons were useful people. In the seventeenth century, George and Thomas Hutcheson founded the Hospital for Poor Boys which had later developed into the famed 'Hutchies' Grammar School in Glasgow. Mary's grandfather Walter was the son of a well-to-do Glasgow businessman but he aspired to the life of an artist and romantically impoverished himself by marrying a poor Highland girl, Jeannie Munro. However, he didn't do badly. He raised seven children and he did well enough as an illustrator to the *Glasgow Herald* and other publications. Working in the pre-photographic age he had to make rapid on-the-spot sketches when on assignments and then rush back to his office to engrave the results.

With the arrival of the press photograph, he found himself redundant and became an art teacher. His work in oils and watercolours was good enough to be exhibited at the Glasgow Art Gallery and other places. But his income dropped to a mere pittance. When his son Jamie (Mary's father) showed signs of inheriting not only the talent but the aspirations of an artist, he was packed off to England to learn to be a gentleman's outfitter. This never appealed to Jamie and he ended up as a traveller for a big cattle feed firm but Mary recalls him as a largely unhappy and frustrated man. He had, in fact, considerable artistic gifts and was never happier than when he was helping Mary with her illustrated school homework.

As a child, Mary and her older sister took a huge pride and delight in two things—their father's noble Scottish brogue and their mother's extraordinary maiden name—Searancke. Two Searanckes certainly crossed from the Low Countries with William III as court physician and court lawyer but Mary later learned that there had been Searanckes in England at least two centuries earlier. They were an influential yeoman family living at Hatfield, Herts. For a woman who has had the mantle of Mrs Grundy thrown upon her, Mary Whitehouse has, at least, chosen inappropriate ancestors. On her father's side—romantic Scottish artists. On her mother's—well, the Searanckes, it transpires, were not only possibly the largest landowners at Hatfield after the Earl of Salisbury but were among the biggest employers in the district. And what did they do? They ran a brewery, and owned eight pubs!

The Searanckes were, beyond argument, strong middle-class; surgeons, clergymen, master bakers and, of course, brewers. In the eighteenth century, they flourished, providing three Mayors of St Albans, a High Sheriff of Hertfordshire and a captain in Nelson's navy. In the nineteenth century, many of them took the fashionable line and went off to the Americas or outposts of Empire; one married a Maori princess. But grandfather Searancke rather ruined the pattern for Mary: a master builder by trade, he died shortly before the birth of his twelfth child leaving a struggling family. A wealthy aunt attempted to adopt Beatrice, Mary's mother, but loneliness and the aunt's insistence that she should turn Catholic meant that the little girl returned to the bosom of her struggling family. And an extraordinary struggle it was, with the three older boys desperately endeavouring to earn the family its crust of bread; one, when aged only ten, sold shoelaces and shoe-polish outside a local shop. In the end, the three boys came through triumphantly and grew up to be successful businessmen in the English Midlands.

Mary's childhood was spent in Chester where the family moved from Shrewsbury during World War One. Their first home there was a large, square, flat-roofed, dark, depressing and damp old house with five blank windows (relics of the eighteenth-century Window Tax) perched high on the City Walls. She, her older sister and her two younger brothers found it all 'very exciting and special', however. They played hopscotch and other games of their own invention on the ancient walls and found the River Dee, with its weir, swans and leaping salmon, a constant delight. But the mists that rose off the river proved harmful to their mother's health and eventually their father was forced to find another much smaller and more cramped house in a different part of the city. Neither Mary nor the other children particularly liked this house but she found compensation in the nearby fields and fondly remembers haymaking, blackberrying and sliding on the frozen ponds in winter.

It was a home, however, not devoid of tragedy. Mary's sister caught polio and was in and out of hospital. As the second child, Mary was expected to relieve her mother of some of the strain of running the household which involved her in such jobs as scrubbing the front of the house and 'whitening' the steps and taking her ailing sister out for a run in her bathchair. Often her mother would order her to take her sister out when Mary had other ideas of how she wanted to spend the time; and so she took a mild sort of revenge. She would race the bathchair violently along the pavements, sister steering the small wheel for dear life, while passers-by scattered in all directions; or sometimes she would allow the bathchair, poor sister still in it, to trundle down the long slope of a railway bridge, Mary racing behind, alert to reach out and grasp its handle if it threatened to overturn.

Her father's job, if neither distinguished nor, because of his artistic leanings, satisfying, was at least well paid. He earned between £10–£20 per week—possibly the equivalent of £100–£200 per week now—but the constant illnesses of mother and elder sister and a bad business speculation left his finances in a precarious state. All the children had to attend the local council school and most of Mary's schoolmates were working-class children with little ambition in life other than to leave school as soon as they reached fourteen. On the whole, despite her Scottish background and the well-known Celtic love of pure learning, Mary was an indifferent pupil. The teachers claimed that she was careless and slapdash, although not without ability. Her parents naturally hoped that she would win a scholarship, but at the age of twelve she failed to do so. But fortunately her marks were good enough to get her into another school from which she was able to attempt the scholarship again at 13; this time she won a bursary which, however, obliged her to take up a teaching career.

At this stage of her development, she was still a careless worker, still slapdash—and pretty rebellious at times. As she puts it herself, 'I was a noncomformist'. She appears also to have been a bit of a tomboy; certainly her mind was concentrated more on fun and games than the hard work necessary to get her matriculation and go on to teaching college. She says that being 'ladylike' held no attractions for her. She refused to 'speak nicely'; neglected to keep the ribbon in her hair properly tied; was constantly in trouble or mischief of one kind or another. Her behaviour was redeemed by her interest in rare stones and pebbles and geology as a general subject and by her skill and talents as a hockey player and athlete (she broke the school's quarter-mile running record). But she remained 'a total mystery and embarrassment' to the headmistress of the Chester and City County School. Both her work and her behaviour tended to be good only in patches—she had an instinct for maths, for example, which often enabled her to get the right answer without the trouble of working it out in detail (a facility, she claims, which has long since deserted her). She had a passion for poetry (and later wrote several pieces) yet both her English grammar and composition were rated indifferent. The drive and energy that were to make her a national character, nevertheless, were already there. However indifferent her academic record—and whatever the reasons—there could be no doubting that this tall long-legged, chubby-faced blonde was no slouch when it came to sports. In an age when girls who went to good schools were still expected to show a bit more initiative than the children of manual labourers, she gravitated towards that pursuit of the genteel commercial classes: tennis. Throughout the summer months, she spent most of her time on a tennis court and at sixteen had developed a powerful serve which could often win her 'love games' against men.

Inspired, she entered local tournaments but her first serious challenge proved too formidable. Matched against the women's Cheshire county champion, she was beaten out of sight. Her performance, nevertheless, was impressive enough to earn her the approval of the tournament officials who suggested to her parents that she should be trained as a county player. James Hutcheson's finances, unfortunately, already had too many calls on them and any vague hopes Mary had of ever appearing on Wimbledon's Centre Court had to be abandoned.

On the whole, then, she had a pretty orthodox upbringing, typical, perhaps of the largest stratum of English society: girl guide, camping, scout dances (her first introduction, as she puts it herself, to the 'social whirl of the late twenties'). She had a bicycle—and with a hunk of Cheshire cheese, a bottle of 'pop' and the inevitable bag of apples, she spent long summer days in the countryside, collecting wild flowers, unusual grasses and leaves and folding them between sheets of paper. A rare pleasure was to cycle home with the sting of cool rain on her face; nor did she ever lose the sense of pleasure at walking through wet grass in her bare feet.

There were boys, of course. At lunchtime each day, the girls, together with the boys from the school next door would squat down along the line that divided the male/female portions of the playing fields and watch cricket. Surreptitious meetings were arranged for after-school and on Saturdays in her last year at school, boys and girls hired boats and went rowing together on the river.

She gained her matriculation by rising at 5 a.m. every day for three weeks before the examination and swotting as hard as she could. That, and deciding that she could afford to flop in one subject: biology. She was so certain that she would do badly in the subject that she laid a sixpenny bet that she would be unable to answer a single question at the exam—and duly collected. Her biology paper was marked 'o out of 300' inducing her harassed headmistress to comment 'You didn't deserve to get School Certificate, let alone Matriculation!' Today she observes with some glee that 'I was held up for years as an example of how *not* to sit an examination.'

It is much too facile to suggest that the present younger generation are incapable of the kind of self-sacrifice and selflessness that characterised the men and women of Mary Whitehouse's youth. All the same, it sounds remarkable that Mary Whitehouse taught at St John's School, Chester, for two years, her first job, for no pay at all. She claims that it was well worthwhile, however; she received an excellent training and became imbued with that enthusiasm for teaching 'which was to stay with me for the rest of my life'.

On the whole it is, perhaps, fair to say that the media (ably abetted by the BBC's Director-General, Sir Hugh Greene) initially underrated both the equipment and abilities of Mary Whitehouse. The original reaction was to see her out among the lunatic fringe. She and the movement which she was eventually to lead at first found themselves patronisingly dismissed as 'non-intellectuals'. In the sense that she never attended Oxbridge, nor, indeed, a redbrick university, this is true. Nevertheless, she had been pitched into a profession where intellectual ideas were what counted and she found herself an emancipated young woman in those gay and nostalgic 'twenties' mixing with young men and women who saw themselves emerging from the stuffy straitjacket of ideas and behaviour typical of the late Victorian and Edwardian periods. She mixed with bright young men and women only too anxious to discuss every aspect of life. 'No subject was taboo,' she insists, 'although I suspect that our conversation was a great deal less obsessed with sex than is usual today.' One of the great talking points, of course, was the Bolshevik coup in Russia—and along with it, such ideas as communism and 'free love'. She and her friends finally decided that extremist ideas were both undesirable and unworkable.

The next stage in her career was a critical one. She went to Crewe to study at the Cheshire County Training College where she was greatly influenced by a brilliant vice-principal, Margaret Phillips. On arrival at College she had been given, as her 'practical' subject, the choice of music or art. Lacking real musical ability though she can still 'bang out' a tune on the piano, she decided upon art—which in view of her family back-ground was a natural choice. She was one of the first to take the new course devised by the Government to train art specialists for secondary schools. But it was to Miss Phillips that she owed the development of a critical appreciation. She was introduced to such figures as Cezak, the Austrian whose ideas greatly in-fluenced the teaching of art to children in pre-war days, and taught to grasp the nature of the work of such a revolutionary artist as Epstein; she was among those who queued to see his *Genesis*.

After College, she had several options open to her. To every-one's astonishment, including her own, she turned her back on teaching in salubrious surroundings and chose, instead, to work with the deprived children of Wednesfield, a suburb of dismal Wolverhampton. She found 'digs' with a young married woman whose husband was in a mental home and who died shortly afterwards. Her salary was a munificent £144 per annum out of which she had five bob left after paying £8.10.0 per month for her 'digs' and £2 for repayment of her College fees. But, as she says now, 'I don't recollect that I missed much'. Despite her grim surroundings and the shortage of cash, she appears to have enjoyed life hugely, partly because of her natural high spirits, partly because of the way the children responded to her teaching, partly because Wednesfield turned out to be full of warm and friendly people. Today, she still thinks of those days as among the happiest periods of her life.

At this stage of her career, Mary Whitehouse was neither priggish nor particularly religious. She had been brought up in a Christian atmosphere and regularly went to church and Sunday school, but at fourteen, she dispensed with both. To her God seemed an irritating irrelevance; religion possibly a myth. She was convinced that she didn't need the help of any Higher Authority in order to run her life. At Training College, her interest in religion returned 'but it was all a bit intellectual and not terribly real to me', although she became President of the Students' Christian Movement. Once out of College, she had 'a whale of a time' and more or less forgot religion again. Her gay, if almost rationally based attitude towards existence, underwent a startling change, however, when she fell in love. To those who can see her only as an obsolete, puritanical old fusspot striving ineffectually, like some provincial Canute, to hold back the incoming tide of our future society, the idea that Mary Whitehouse once found herself emotionally involved with a married man must seem bizarre. She will not discuss the details and will say nothing more than that it was a period of 'unhappiness and conflict'. But it was at this juncture that the solace of religion gave her life a new twist and purpose.

Some time before, a girl friend, a Methodist, took her along to an upstairs room in the Wolverhampton YMCA to hear some young men belonging to the Oxford Group talk about what they described as 'life changing'. Among them was a certain Ernest Whitehouse—although it would be two more years before she even spoke to him. She listened to their message, found their demeanour and arguments impressive but was too pre-occupied at the time to pay much attention to them. In the wake of her unhappy love experience, however, her thoughts turned again to the idea of religion and in 1935 she became a member of the Wolverhampton branch of the Oxford Group. 'It is now many years since I asked God to take my life and use it, and, although they have held many experiences of sorrow as well as joy, they have been wholly satisfying,' she says.

Profound and lasting though her 'conversion' was, there were other and more practical concerns of interest to her in the Wolverhampton group. There was Ernest. They were thrown more and more together (even her tennis had to take a back seat) and they carried on their courtship at branch meetings and while travelling around the Midlands speaking in churches and at other organised gatherings as part of an Oxford Group team. In due course, membership of the Oxford Group led to membership of Moral Rearmament, based on the ideas of an American, Dr Frank Buchman, and fostered in this country by Peter Howard, a journalist. Mary and Ernest worked with Moral Rearmament during the War and afterwards, though they ceased to be involved to any extent when Ernest had a long illness in 1956.

Mary Whitehouse insists that she never became very deeply involved in Moral Rearmament, mainly because it was less concerned with group exhortation and involvement than the Oxford Group. She joined it, she explains, principally because of its similiarities with the Oxford Group but agrees that part of its attitude could be considered political. 'It was not a question of backing or attacking any individual or any political party but of insisting that the quality of a person's individual behaviour and way of living was vital to the way the country behaved as a whole—which I still believe profoundly, anyway. It could be called political in that it exposed communist infiltration of British institutions—which is the genesis of the antagonism that has been shown to it.'

Marriage had to be put off until March, 1940, owing to the long illness, culminating in the death of, Ernest's mother. Ernest at this time worked with his father, an industrial coppersmith who had adapted an instrument used by brewers to enable farmers to cool and preserve their milk; over the years the business had expanded from a small backstreet workshop into a flourishing concern making different instruments used in milk refrigeration and copper water cylinders.

Their first son, Paul, was born in 1941 and after this Mary had to face up to her first really difficult period and make her first really difficult decision. She became pregnant with twins but had to spend several months in bed and as her condition worsened she was advised by her doctor to have an abortion. Abortion, naturally, was anathema to her—and though the babies were born, they did not live. A second son, Richard, was born in 1945 and it was while he was still a baby that Mary Whitehouse entered public life. Touched by the stories of the sufferings then being experienced by the German civilian population after the end of the war, she and a friend decided to try to help. They began by collecting clothes and other goods from their friends and then, with her baby in her arms, Mary addressed a public meeting which she and her friend had organised in the Wolverhampton Library. To her astonishment and, she admits, horror—although she was grateful for the publicity—the local evening newspaper carried a banner headline next day: MOTHER PLEADS FOR EUROPE'S SUFFERING CHILDREN. She felt so embarrassed that she was unable to set foot outside the house for a fortnight. Even today, although she appears on the surface to be a supremely self-assured person, she is according to her friends a very sensitive woman who is easily hurt or embarrassed and who has had to struggle hard to overcome a measure of timidity. Nonetheless, the publicity was of immense help and the effort continued for several months with gifts flowing in from all sides. In view of the intense hatred which had been whipped up in Britain during the five long years of War, the response was a tribute to the people of Wolverhampton. As for Mary Whitehouse, her action compels our admiration, particularly as she was a sick woman and had to carry a baby about.

Her third son, Christopher, was born in 1946—and the

family was completed shortly afterwards when the Whitehouses fostered Mary's three-month-old niece after the death of her sister-in-law in South Africa. They lived at this time on an uncompleted pre-war estate at Lower Penn which had only four houses. The estate was surrounded by open fields providing the children with an excellent playground. Work with the Oxford Group and Moral Rearmament continued—indeed, Mary's connection with the latter ceased only when she began her Clean-Up TV campaign in the 1960s. She had fewer and fewer opportunities to play tennis but Ernest, a keen rock climber, often took their eldest son Paul climbing in the hills of Snowdonia. The boy became an adept mountaineer: he once scared the life out of Mary when she caught him perched on the chimney stack of a neighbouring house.

Religion, of course, was a dominating factor in the family's life. Those virtues sometimes hailed in England as part of 'middle-class morality', i.e. thrift and education, were encouraged. All three boys studied beyond the normal elementary curriculum. Paul went to the University of Birmingham and Richard to Birmingham College of Art. A holiday in 1948 in a seaside boarding house proved such torture that thenceforward all holidays were spent in a converted bus parked near the Barmouth estuary in Wales. While the children splashed in the sea, Mary sat quietly by, writing poetry. If scarcely a flashy existence, she recalls it as a deeply satisfying one.

Neither she nor Ernest were ardent cinemagoers; in fact, they rarely attended the cinema at all. 'They're not cinema people, they don't like films,' says youngest son Christopher, now on the staff of the *Birmingham Post*. Nor were the Whitehouses great socialisers—although at this time Mary sometimes had friends in for barbecues in the back garden. She was nothing like the supremely self-confident person she appears today. She was even-tempered; laughed at life's little absurdities, but rarely, if ever, told a joke; and was never sentimental—'she's never been silly about things', says Christopher. 'For instance, she didn't

show any particular distress when our Welsh sheepdog died. And
I particularly remember that she didn't cry when her mother
died. She's too level-headed to allow her emotions to get over-
heated.'

For all her latent strength of character, she was not the
dominant figure in the household. 'Father was that,' says
Christopher. 'He was never a domineering man, by any means
—but the household roles were sharply defined. Mother organised the house—on the whole she was very efficient until her
Clean-Up TV campaign began—I'd say she's less efficient now.
And if she's not a great organiser in the technical sense, she's
capable of organising her life so that things get organised. But it
was my father who made—and still makes—all the major
decisions; that is about moving house, about food, about money
and so on. He's the kind of man who only *does* things in life
because he considers them useful—and these views extend to
everything, so that he takes great care over all his decisions. In
many respects my parents are complete opposites. Mother
doesn't feel quite the same way about things. On another level
I wouldn't say she was rash—she doesn't spend foolishly,
buying up earrings and things like that although she's quite
fashion conscious—by the way she can never throw anything
away. She's less careful and deliberate in her approach to
things.'

There were further troubles. The adopted baby became ill
and Mary had to take her to hospital regularly for check-ups.
This always proved a weary safari—first the walk to the bus stop,
then a journey into the town centre; then a further walk with a
baby in one arm, a two-year-old son in the other and a four-
year-old clinging to her skirts. The difficulties—exacerbated by
having to push the pram over unmade roads—led to a move and
they settled down in a large Victorian house in Merridale Road
close to the town centre and with a large garden—'big enough
for cricket' and an orchard plus an old fountain which the
eldest boy soon turned into a fine pond.

Next door but one lived Enoch Powell and his family. The two small Powell daughters could be seen watching with interest as the Whitehouse children built a 'tree house' in the garden. The Whitehouses, for their part watched Mr Powell plant out lettuce seedlings in his small patch of garden but they were less than impressed with the way he handled his only apple tree, part of which overhung their garden. Characteristically, instead of picking the fruit carefully from the tree, he grabbed hold of the tree and *shook the fruit down*! Mary Whitehouse remembers three workmen repairing her property who made 'unprintable remarks' about 'that man over the wall' who hadn't even the commonsense to pick his fruit properly.

Sickness continued to afflict them. Richard, when six years old, picked up an infection which so crippled him with rheumatism that he had to lie in bed for several months on end and was unable to return to full-time schooling until he was twelve. Young Christopher was playing in an outhouse when a spirit level exploded and damaged his right eye. It seemed certain, at first, that he would lose his eye.

It suits Mary Whitehouse to believe that God intervened—although she makes no direct claim for any kind of miracle. To a Christian, of course, this claim will appear anything but absurd. The whole episode only served to reinforce Mary Whitehouse's profound belief in the power of prayer. A large network of friends, contacted by telephone, offered up prayers for the boy. The eye was saved and only a partial loss of sight resulted. Three years later, when Christopher was finally discharged from hospital, the surgeon observed, 'this has been the most remarkable case I've ever handled.'

She enjoyed a modest first triumph. To her astonishment, in Coronation Year 1953, Mary Whitehouse found herself broadcasting on BBC Woman's Hour on the eve of Queen Elizabeth's Coronation. She had been so impressed by the new monarch's first Christmas broadcast after her accession in 1952 that she had written down some thoughts on how people could help the

Queen and sent them to the BBC. Her ideas coincided with a
BBC search for a woman 'who had been changed' by the
Queen's broadcast and so 'A Housewife's Thoughts on the Eve
of the Coronation' was broadcast.

But rather incredibly the vigorous, alert, healthy woman we
see today had become a chronic invalid. The strain of coping
with the children plus certain kidney trouble laid her low most
winters during which she usually spent several weeks in bed. It
culminated in a kidney infection which kept her in bed for fourteen weeks at a stretch. Although friends helped, the burden of
running the house fell upon Ernest. When convalescent, Mary's
mother took her for a six-week-holiday to the Canaries and she
returned tanned and seemingly fit; but although she had
recovered according to her doctors, her stamina had been im-
paired and housework rapidly pulled her down again. A daily
help was the obvious solution but Ernest's income could not run
to such luxuries.

She decided that a part-time job teaching art was the answer
and finally, in 1957, landed a post at a school nearby where she
brought 'open approach' to her teaching. Her idea was not so
much to impose disciplines and conformities on the children
as to break the rigid mould of instruction and instead open
their minds—and thereby their enthusiasms—to the possibilities of being able to express themselves by painting or drawing.

There were to be more changes of residence; first in 1956 a
move to a fine house in Upper Penn on the outskirts of Wolverhampton; then, in 1960, to the picturesque Shropshire village of
Claverley, six miles from the industrial wasteland. By this time,
her Paul was at University and her second son, Richard, at
Birmingham College of Art. She found herself with time on her
hands and finally sought—and obtained—an appointment at
Madeley Secondary Modern School. At an age when most
people usually feel that the best part of their lives are over and
that their greatest achievements are past, she unknowingly stood

on the threshold of a revolutionary change that was to bring her, if not, alas, great fortune, certainly a respectable, if totally un-expected fame and the satisfaction of a sense of mission and purpose that could almost be compared to that of St Joan of Arc.

CHAPTER FOUR

David and Goliath

In May 1973, Mary Whitehouse was in hospital suffering from malaria contracted during a holiday in Gambia. Among the many letters from well-wishers was one, unsigned, black on one side and grey on the other, expressing the sender's sincere hope that *she would never come out of hospital alive*!

The campaign that was to make Mary Whitehouse a British national figure and to earn her the attention of the Pope and of a US Presidential Commission on Obscenity and Pornography was launched, she insists, with only one aim: to protect children. 'When we began,' she says, 'I was deeply and angrily concerned with the impact of all this filth pouring out from television and other sources on the children I was teaching—very much more than I was concerned with the attacks on my own beliefs.'

The early days brought incalculable agonies. 'I've always been sensitive about what people feel about me—it's always been one of my characteristics,' she says. 'I didn't like being described as a "hypocritical old bitch" by the late Sir Gerald Nabarro MP in a programme chaired by Ned Sherrin. The idea that I was some sort of fuddy-duddy, too, hurt me. I suffered a lot from tension and worry for several years—I'd actually get tummy upsets. In the beginning, it was very difficult; I had to steel myself even to talk to the press.

'The worst was to feel that I and all that I stood for were so *vulnerable*. I seemed to have enemies everywhere—there seemed no person in any position of power or influence, no institution of any kind, which was prepared to offer me any protection. I don't think I would have suffered so much had the questions I

43

raised been allowed to come to the surface and been dealt with
objectively—on their merits. Instead, it was a process of distortion and—well, almost defamation.

'I remember when I first went on TV on one of those *Talkback*
programmes and I made the suggestion that there should be a
Broadcasting Council (similar to the Press Council which
monitors the behaviour of the press and either exonerates or
censures it). It was as though I were suggesting mass murder or
something equally reprehensible. Everybody in the studio was
against me—they pounced on me and tore me to shreds—I'm
quite sure the TV people had the panel packed with their
supporters. Next morning, the *Daily Mirror* ran the headline,
DECLINE AND FALL OF SUPER CRITIC.'

There never came a point, however, at which she felt she
could not carry on the work. 'I always felt a commitment—a
deep sense that this was a job I had to do. I can truthfully say
that I never reached a stage where I felt I couldn't take any
more.' One of her mentors, one of the first men of authority and
influence to offer her any kind of consolation and advice, was
William Deedes, Conservative MP for Ashford, Kent and
journalist. Bill Deedes, of course, is not the kind of man who, in
any real sense of the term, could be called a Mary Whitehouse
supporter. But as a senior politician and journalist of experience,
his advice is continually being sought from different quarters.
He has specialised to some extent in the wider implications of
obscenity and pornography and its effects on British society. If
not entirely dispassionate, he is at least an experienced public
figure. When an upset Mary, feeling very downcast and de-
pressed, once telephoned him, he met her in Fleet Street and
warned her, 'Now listen, my dear, you are inevitably going to
have this kind of attack. They're going to tear you to shreds.
You've got to get to a certain depth of despair, to be pushed
down so far, before the great British public is going to wake up
and say, "This woman really can't be as bad as she's made out
to be."'

It was the very excesses of her critics that eventually showed her how she could turn attacks to her own advantage. She is not a Zen Buddhist, has no idea of Yin and Yang, has never even heard of Bruce Lee, the kung fu expert whose whole 'art' was based on the principle of using an opponent's strength to defeat him. She simply hit on the technique accidentally and has been using it ever since. When William Hardcastle, the radio interviewer, wrote an article in the *Listener* which she considered 'full of inaccuracies,' explaining that 'What was really irritating was that whatever I said or did made not the slightest bit of difference, people always insisted on making statements which were at total variance with our view'—she rang up the editor and asked for the right to reply. To her astonishment, the editor agreed and offered her the 'same amount of space in which to state your case'. She says, 'There was a deliberate attempt during those days to give us (The Clean-Up TV campaign and later NVALA) an inaccurate image which used to get me down more than anything else. But once the *Listener* agreed to print my reply, I realised that attacks are things you can use positively. They can be used to transform the whole situation. I think you could say that I am no longer troubled by attacks—because they provide me with new platforms.'

Her early efforts to alert what remained of Christian England to the attacks being made on a morality that it had long taken for granted were greeted with something much worse than mere distortion or verbal onslaughts. There was a spate of threatening telephone calls; sometimes she was awakened at three in the morning to listen to a blood-curdling warning; it was impossible to dismiss all these calls as the work of cranks and the police advised her not to stay in the house alone at nights. Then there were obscene letters by the dozen (fortunately both calls and letters have now almost ceased). Attempts were also made to discredit her by luring her sons to orgies on the pretext that they were invited to Christmas or birthday parties. Later the decision of Sir Hugh Carleton-Greene, ex-Director-General of the BBC, to hang a painting apparently a full frontal nude of Mrs White-house (with no fewer than *five* breasts) in his home became an act of psychological assault. Yet, in a sense, nearly everything seems insignificant compared with the effect on herself and on her husband of a BBC TV programme in 1964.

In the end, Mary Whitehouse was to extract a degree of amusement from *Swizzlewick*, a series which fairly obviously set out to make fun of her. The first she heard of this series, written by David Turner, an individual with whom she had already crossed swords, was when a friend rang her one day in August to tell her that she was in 'this week's issue of the *Radio Times*'.

'Oh, don't be daft!' replied Mary in her best Cheshire accent.

'Well, your hat's there, even if you're not,' said her friend.

She found a picture of her current hat on an inside page together with a rather vague representation of her features. The whole ensemble was meant to represent a Mrs Smallgood, 'heroine' of a 'freedom from sex' campaign which had been launched in mythical Swizzlewick. One of the chief characters was a Councillor Salt (chairman of her Clean-Up TV campaign was a Councillor Pepper). As the series got under way a character called Ernie, a postman, was eventually introduced. Could all this be coincidence, wondered the Whitehouses?— after all the name of their cottage was 'Postman's Piece'.

The series was transmitted at a time when the Whitehouses were undergoing a severe personal crisis. On a dark, foggy night the previous November Ernest had been driving home along a narrow, winding Shropshire lane when, as he turned a corner, he saw a bundle lying in the road, picked out in his headlamps. It seemed like a sack and it was not until his car bumped over the inert figure of a young airman who had deliberately placed himself there that Ernest realised something was wrong. Fortunately, the young man had left a note declaring that he intended to commit suicide and the inquest jury completely exonerated Ernest. Nevertheless, his nightmare memories refused to leave him and eventually he collapsed with nervous strain and had to undergo psychiatric treatment.

One evening Mary Whitehouse watched with fascination as Ernie the postman appeared on the screen. This time the poor man was not well—so he was brought into the house and laid down on a sofa. Then it turned out that he was suffering from guilt feelings as a result of hitting a dog with a football! The solution?—why not a little psychological treatment, a little hypnosis?

Fortunately for Ernest, he did not see the whole of the episode but when, many months later after he had recovered, Mary told him about the parody he was very angry that she had not protested to the BBC at the time. She wonders how the producer and the writer came to know about Ernest's illness which not many people outside her immediate circle knew about.

In the end *Swizzlewick* helped Mary Whitehouse and her cause far more than it damaged them. The series was meant to be a skit on local councils but was considered almost libellous and so wide of the mark that it caused an uproar among local government and council officials.

The local Wolverhampton paper described *Swizzlewick* as 'salacious and sordid' and added that 'not only was the sex angle overplayed but also the rumblings of corrupt practice and colour prejudice'. The *Guardian*, hardly an arch-conservative paper, considered the programme 'a new low in tastelessness'. The *Catholic Pictorial* talked about 'obese offerings of adolescent smut'. Mary Whitehouse herself is prepared to allow that the BBC's own justification for the programme—that it was meant to take the lid off council pomposity and encourage people to laugh at themselves—had merit. She insists that she never tried to discourage the pricking of pomposities or the pretensions of local tyrants—although, on the whole, she sees council officials and officers as hard-working and responsible men engaged in a generally thankless task. However, she had no doubt that the programme was a deliberate attempt to ridicule her and her TV

clean-up campaign and when offered the opportunity to hit back
seized it with both hands.

On August 24 1964, the television correspondent of the
Birmingham Mail had some caustic things to say of the *Swizzlewick* episode due to be broadcast the following Tuesday. The
next day, Mrs Whitehouse was offered, 'quite out of the blue
and by somebody I did not know' a transcript of the controversial episode. To this day, she refuses to reveal the name of the
person who gave it to her, other than to insist that she did not
obtain it from a member of the *Birmingham Post*. The episode, by
Mrs Whitehouse's standards, was far from edifying. In one scene
a councillor is shown coming out of the room of Blousie, a
prostitute, with his clothes in disarray.

She sent the script to the Postmaster-General. A friendly MP
gave her a special code number; she took the script to the Head
Postmaster at Wolverhampton and the material was in the
hands of the PMG inside a few hours. Then newspapers were
alerted as to what was going on.

'Will you know if any cuts are made?' a reporter asked her.

'At least I'll have a general idea,' she replied.

In the event, transmission time was cut by two and a half
minutes or the equivalent of about 300 words. Out entirely went
the scene where the councillor is shown coming out of Blousie's
room. Next day the press had a field day—'What happened to
Blousie?' they demanded. The result was the resignation of
David Turner, writer of the series, on the grounds of 'unethical
cuts' and the termination of the series.

According to Mary Whitehouse, the Director-General returned from his holidays in a rare fury at learning that she had
managed to get hold of the script. An inquiry was instituted but
the secret still remains locked in her breast. She believes that
it was as a consequence of this that word went out to BBC
personnel warning them not to have anything to do with her—
either professionally or socially. If such a directive were issued,
the reason, of course, need not necessarily have been as sinister

as Mrs Whitehouse sees it. Sir Hugh Greene, indeed, may have been genuinely angry but it could well be argued that no corporation can be expected to feel comfortable conducting its business with people walking in off the streets to query its decisions. The results of this case, however, appear to have been more farcical than sinister. BBC men had even to slip out of innocuous social functions once they discovered Mrs Whitehouse was present. Yet she still somehow managed to keep in contact with many BBC personnel. Some, she claims, telephoned her anonymously; others stayed behind at her meetings until everyone else had gone, then approached her and introduced themselves as 'from the BBC'. She found it all an absurd and idiotic game and had little difficulty circumventing the BBC switchboard and getting directly through to producers of programmes to which she objected.

Sir Hugh Greene may have underestimated Mary Whitehouse and the large number of people who eventually rallied round her. He instinctively relegated her and her followers to the periphery of cranks. At the time, particularly in view of his radical ideas of how the BBC should develop, she must have appeared as just one more irritant: yet another voice among many thousands complaining about something or clamouring to have their say. It has been argued that he could have easily defused the whole Mary Whitehouse phenomenon by inviting her to Broadcasting House to calm and reassure her. Instead, however, he chose to ignore her and met her challenge head on.

There were individuals within the BBC, nevertheless, who practised a slightly different approach and who believe that contact with her had a mutually beneficial effect. Anthony Smith, the documentary producer, who once ran the current affairs programme *24 Hours*, says that he had little option but to talk to Mary Whitehouse who found ways of getting through to him on the telephone. However busy, he always elected to 'take her on' and debate any points she raised with him. He made a specific policy of arguing her down; 'I was never the first to put the phone down,' he says. Mary herself admits that when she first obtruded onto the TV and radio scene she was completely naive and had very little understanding of the pressures and problems connected with programme making.

'I didn't understand, for instance,' she says, 'that a producer might make a genuine attempt to get a "balanced" panel and either find that the hundred per cent right "mix" was not available or that when they actually got talking, people revealed surprising opinions or unexpected inadequacies.' Anthony Smith, who now considers many of the points Mary Whitehouse has been campaigning for are valid—especially with regard to 'access' and 'censorship by exclusion', nevertheless believes that contact with a wider world has also changed Mary Whitehouse; and she agrees.

'I think she began as quite a sanctimonious figure,' Smith says, 'but there's been an enormous change since she became a public figure. People who knew her at the beginning tended to find her a bit too good to be true. That, I think, is not valid any longer. There is no denying of course, that she has "star" quality—I think she could have proved this in any field. She unquestionably exercises real influence on people who meet her. It's not that you become inhibited in her presence—it's just that you don't seem to want to swear, to think—well, the kind of evil thoughts that most people are always thinking. But just as soon as you're outside the magic circle of her influence, I find, you immediately return to normal.

'I think this is the whole problem—and has been at the root of the problem since the beginning. The whole difficulty with Mary Whitehouse and her movement is that they have invented a scale of values which operate for and in her group but which neither apply nor can be applied to the outside world.'

Today Mary Whitehouse tends to see Anthony Smith and others like him, as partial 'converts' to her cause. She and Smith have met frequently, particularly since he quit his job at the BBC to do research at Oxford University and they often present papers on TV at seminars, although never, of course, jointly. They talk together in a friendly way on the telephone and once when I was visiting her house Smith rang up to invite her to a cricket match at Minster Lovell, in which many of the old satirical TV buffs such as Ned Sherrin and David Frost were due to take part.

Yet Smith's stand in reality still remains poles apart from that of Mary Whitehouse, though they do share one area of common agreement. Both see the people actually working in TV at producer, writer and the higher administrative levels as an elitist body; they see them as an introverted group of individuals who, whatever their talents and abilities, nevertheless tend to be isolated from ordinary people. Smith agrees with Mary Whitehouse that the existence of such a tightly knit, privileged little group is unhealthy and sees a desperate need for easier access for the public, for a *great deal* more public participation. Yet he wants *more* freedom for TV and inclines towards the view that, for all her protestations about the need for greater public participation and access to the medium, for less 'censorship by exclusion', if Mary's ideas and value judgements were accepted by the BBC and IBA, it would lead to *less* rather than to *more*, liberty. It is an argument that is not easy for Mary Whitehouse to discount; though whatever her original objections to some of the material broadcast by the television authorities, the balance of her argument today is that when controversial material is screened, there should be simply an opportunity to express opposition. Her objective is now that, when humanists and others with a pronounced anti-Christian bias are allowed to air their opinions, the opposite view should also be made available so that the public hears both sides of the question. Yet for all the sincerity with which she holds forth on the need for a greater need for 'access', she would still, if she had her way, exclude material such as the *Casanova* series. Indeed, having watched a repeat of the first episode in 1974, she at once sat down and wrote

a protest to Sir Michael Swann, chairman of the BBC, objecting that the Corporation was projecting a *Playboy* philosophy.

'I wrote that the idea that the BBC (of all institutions) should
involve young girls in some of the scenes and dialogue was
simply outrageous. Some of the conversation between Casanova
and the girls was beyond belief! And you had scene after scene
showing girl after girl nude to the waist.' She adds, 'Nor is it any
use arguing that the series was taken from a written classic. Books
and TV are not the same thing. When you read something, you
can interpret it with your own imagination—in a sense, you can
censor or control your own thoughts and emotions. But TV—or
films for that matter—is something different. If something is
spelt out explicitly on the screen, there is no escape from it. You
are a prisoner of what you see—what is thrust at you; and to that
extent your mind is corrupted.'

Anthony Smith would not deny the impact of TV but he
would certainly part company with Mary Whitehouse over
excluding *Casanova*. Feeling that he is viewing TV from perhaps
a wider perspective, he sees Mary Whitehouse as 'an evil influence'. I found it hard to credit that a woman who believes so
profoundly in God and high moral standards should be castigated as 'evil'; so difficult in fact, that I queried Smith's use of
the word. He repeated his charge and explained what he meant.
In essence, it amounts to a persuasive and almost convincing
argument and many would share his view.

He sees Sir Hugh Greene as anything but the sinister figure
Mary Whitehouse pictures him. To her, Greene was a master
propagandist who having helped to overthrow Nazism put his
esoteric talents to work, after the war, into the business of
suborning the British way of life. Anthony Smith, on the other
hand, sees Greene as a giant influence for freedom—a man who,
in the light of a rapidly changing society, decided to let everyone
have a say. He does not deny that Left-wingers 'perhaps got
things too much their own way' and agrees that there was a
period when it was quite impossible to get a serious right-wing

play on BBC television. Despite the fact that the current drama series *Play for Today* still constantly reflects a left-wing bias and that there is little sign of any other opinion being allowed an airing, he feels that the left-wing grip has been broken. He sees the great 'satirical' wave as certainly finished and he makes the point that most of the 'satirists' had public school backgrounds and were conservatives politically. Those people who felt offended by some of the 'satirical' programmes were perhaps under the impression that the participants were a bunch of knaves, determined to destroy the democratic British process. They may now, in the light of Smith's observations, take the view that the group were merely fools who had no real idea of the implications of their folly. Anthony Smith insists that all cultures must change or die and that there was little truly subversive about the 'satirists'; instead they were merely performing a necessary function in helping British society to adjust to the new circumstances in which it found itself.

Mary Whitehouse did not—and still does not—like what those TV 'satirists' had to offer. In this, she finds herself separated from many of her sympathisers. Malcolm Muggeridge has written: 'I cannot accept her blanket disapproval of *That Was The Week That Was* and the other Late Shows which followed. It has always seemed to me that humour is the great moral prophylatic, and that what is really funny—as quite a high proportion of the numbers of these shows were—cannot be objectionable. As far as I know, it has never been suggested that Rabelais is pornographic even though four-letter words crop up in his pages more frequently than in *Lady Chatterley's Lover*, his art is born in laughter. . . .' Nevertheless, if Muggeridge had to choose between Mary Whitehouse and Kenneth Tynan, the first man on television to use the four-letter word for the sexual act, he elects to join Mary's side; if it were a question of either VALA or *Oh, Calcutta* (a sexy stage entertainment sponsored or engineered by Tynan) he had no doubt, either, where he stood— he would be for VALA.

William Deedes reflects an objective, almost unemotional approach to the problem. He believes that one of the essentials of social stability is the need to make sure that 'too large a minority is not allowed to form who might feel that their objections about something, their feelings about something, are going by default. It is really no good ignoring the fact that some —let's call it a minority in this country, for the sake of argument —are offended by certain aspects of pornography and indecency in what passes for entertainment today—by the liberties taken by television and by stage and screen. If such a minority is not represented by somebody, you've always got to take into account the possible risk that some day somebody may decide that the best thing to do is to bung a brick through a cinema window or tear down the poster of a nude lady being whipped by a nude man and reckon that was their contribution—or, as the cowboys used to do in America years ago, start firing through the screen'. Deedes is here talking about Mary Whitehouse and the need for her and for VALA—yet it is the kind of argument that Sir Hugh Greene and his supporters would have unquestionably employed regarding the need to allow minority left-wing or even near-anarchical views an airing on television. However, an airing of minority views which leads increasingly to a monopoly of such views—a constant forcing of the line of tolerance about both politics and those moral values originally meant to protect the individual against murder, violence, rape, robbery, theft and all other enemies of civilised behaviour—are by no means the same thing.

It was precisely because of this tendency that Mary White-house, driven to extreme indignation by what she considered the continuing excesses of the BBC, decided to do something about it all. However one views it, it was an astonishing decision—and perhaps no one has been more astonished than Mary White-house herself at the success that has attended her efforts. The idea of David against Goliath had never occurred to her—and although the Philistine has been far from laid low, it cannot be said that he has not been forced to tread a great deal more warily. For many people up and down Britain, Mary Whitehouse has by now exerted a powerful and beneficial effect. Some, indeed, are already prepared to breathe her name alongside those of Elizabeth Fry's and Florence Nightingale's.

CHAPTER FIVE

The Birth of 'Clean-up TV'

'You've got to remember the climate of the times,' insists Mary Whitehouse. 'Religion, the idea of God, Christianity in particular, were very much under attack. It is one thing to argue that Robinson's *Honest to God* was a necessary intellectual and theological exercise—but the whole effect on the ordinary man and woman was that God was dead; that there was a New Morality about and that it was justified. In those days, the whole of religious broadcasting seemed to lend its weight to this New Morality. *Meeting Point* programmes seemed loaded on the side of the radical clergymen who appeared to be having it all their own way. I think that what we did changed all that. Today I consider religious broadcasting both on TV and radio very fine, indeed.

'You've got to remember that when we began, we were very ordinary people. We still are, of course. We had absolutely no experience of the world of the media and no understanding of the deeper ramifications of our move. It was simply a spontaneous grassroots movement of people who shared a common concern. I've never set out to work for Christian values alone—even now, we have a number of people on VALA's executive committee who would not call themselves Christian. Certainly, the majority of the close group are Christian—but that's not an issue. What we are concerned with are moral values alone. A difficulty, of course, is that our society is primarily based on the Christian ethic—that is, our laws, our ideas of justice, our ideas of the rights of the individual. And once you attack either Christianity or the democratic structure, then as we saw—and still see it—you are attacking both.

'We don't—and never did—see ourselves as anything more than one voice speaking on this whole question of morals and values in the country. We are not trying to *impose* our will or our views on others. What we are trying to do is to battle for our own views—which we believe is what democracy is all about. I'm constantly saying at meetings that the last thing I'm interested in is giving my life to persuading people to agree with me. What is important is that everybody speaks out and makes their voice heard. It so happens that my experience leads me to believe that most people would be on the side of responsible morality. What we're suffering from is an *imbalance*. One of the most frightening things in Britain today is that those who are against censorship, insist they want no censorship, are the very people who will go to any lengths to silence us.

'I've never said—and am not saying now—that the voices of anarchy and chaos are not entitled to put their point of view. The fact is that they *have been* putting it—and still are putting it. Our battle has been—and still is—to get the other side of the coin heard.'

This view of her 12-year campaign reflects, as Mary Whitehouse herself admits, a rather more sophisticated attitude towards her role than the one with which she started out. As she says herself, her movement began as a rather crude and spontaneous reaction to 'what was being spewed out on television'.

After her visit to Broadcasting House in the summer of 1963, followed by her interviews with the Bishop of Hereford, Jasper More, MP for Ludlow, Enoch Powell and the Midlands representative of the Independent Television Authority, Mrs Whitehouse had, naively as she admits, concluded that TV programmes would begin to reflect a recognition of the fact that many people considered a great deal of the material highly offensive. Instead, the programmes appeared to get even more outrageous. But, as she puts it herself, 'there was still hope.' The BBC's Charter was due for renewal at the beginning of 1964.

She had some vague idea, apparently, that Parliament might try to put a bridle on the BBC in the wake of the uproar, even furore, that had been caused by Sherrin's *That Was The Week That Was*, a television programme that, to put it mildly, was highly irreverent. This programme and its successors hardly allowed such punctilious matters as tastelessness to stand in the way of what they wanted to go on about. Mary Whitehouse asserts that 'women's organisations, magistrates, Church leaders, feature writers and public and private figures joined in the chorus of protest'—a chorus which Sir Hugh Greene labelled 'the lunatic fringe'. Conversely certain organs of opinion felt compelled to label some items in the programme offensive. The late *Daily Sketch* found one show 'as smutty as a train window in a Crewe railway siding'. *Time and Tide*, the weekly magazine, thought the programme 'sinister'. The *Daily Telegraph* considered it 'raised questions of taste, fairness, propriety and even libel'. These journals represented a conservative view on almost every aspect of British society, not just television. Sherrin, Frost and company, if they set out to offend people and institutions, succeeded admirably. Looking back now, it is hard to think of any institution they did not aim a missile at. Every known form of pomposity and pretension was pricked and thoroughly punctured. But how brilliant and amusing it all was! How glorious to find at least one television programme emerging from the era of warmed-up music-hall and exploring the mindlessness of much contemporary British thinking. Instead, dazzling, intelligent, witty conversationalists thrusting epigrams at each other with speed and fluency made one feel one was listening to a set-to between Oscar Wilde and George Bernard Shaw. With considerable justification, Sir Hugh Greene could announce, when the show was taken off towards the end of 1963, 'I enjoyed it. It was very good. It was positive and exhilarating. I have no objection to the language used.' It was a view with which a large proportion of the population would agree. Mistakes there may have been. Not everything accorded with the very high standards the show set itself. But taken by and large, its numerous gaffes and lapses could be forgiven; it was adult entertainment in the very best sense of the word and a reminder of how ingenious, inventive and sophisticated much of English society really is.

Mary Whitehouse did not like it then—nor does she like it any the better now. At the time, in common with many people in the island, she believed that when the moment came to renew or cancel the BBC's charter that members of the Government and other Westminster politicians who had taken much stick from Frost and his merry band would exact a telling revenge. To her astonishment, Jasper More, her local MP, rang her up one day to announce that Parliament had renewed the Corporation's charter for a further twelve years.

'What are you going to do now?' inquired the MP.

Her answer sprang from 'the depths of my disappointment'. Without dwelling too much on what she was saying, she replied, 'Well, there's nothing left, is there, but for the women of the country to rise up and say that we have not borne our children nor built our homes to have them undermined like this.'

'I think you're right,' said More. 'I'm sure nothing else will do.'

That, she believes, was the moment when her Clean-Up TV campaign, later to develop into the National Viewers' and Listeners' Association, was born.

It began more literally with a phone call to Mrs Norah Buckland, an old friend who was wife of the then Rector of Longton, Stoke-on-Trent. Mrs Buckland had three children, was a member of the Mothers' Union, had given evidence to a British Medical Association Committee on young people and venereal diseases, and had spent a great deal of her time visiting schools and lecturing on 'The Way to Happiness'. Mothers had complained to her that the BBC slipped objectionable material into plays in such a way as to give the impression that this was normal behaviour. Alarmed by the apparent lack of moral

standards that lay behind certain documentaries, Mrs Buckland
had preceded Mary Whitehouse in asking the BBC to receive a
deputation; the request had been refused, albeit courteously.
Together the two women decided that as individual protests
were invariably met with a reply which suggested that it was
they, the mothers, who were out of step with contemporary
mores rather than the BBC, concerted action might be more
successful. With the assistance of their husbands, the two women
got down to the task of drawing up a Manifesto.

Its tone was straightforward and unambiguous. It objected to
the 'propaganda of disbelief, doubt and dirt' broadcast by the
BBC; complained that the Corporation employed 'people whose
ideas and advice pander to the lowest in human nature and
accompany this with a stream of suggestive and erotic plays' and
declared that the women of Britain who believed in a Christian
way of life demanded a radical change of policy by the BBC,
together with programmes 'which build character instead of
destroying it' and which sustained faith in God.

To be fair to Mrs Whitehouse and her husband, they are the
first to admit that their Manifesto, by any objective judgement,
was both unfair and inaccurate, when the *total* output of the
BBC was considered. Whatever the excesses of certain programmes there could be no disputing the extraordinary quality
and excellence of the Corporation's output which justifiably
earned it the title of the world's best broadcasting network and
added lustre to the quality of British life. While admitting to
some faults in the Manifesto, Mary Whitehouse still feels that
the BBC were unlikely to respond to any ordinary courteous
form of protest, particularly those people within the BBC who
were 'hellbent on the destruction of accepted standards'.

She and Norah Buckland decided to have 2,000 copies of the
Manifesto printed and to seek twenty signatures on each,
believing that a petition signed by 40,000 people would have
some influence on the BBC hierarchy. It didn't. Baffled as to
what to do next, they took the advice of Birmingham Councillor

J. W. Pepper, who was already running his own local TV campaign, and got in touch with the *Birmingham Evening Mail* who sent a reporter along to see Mary at Claverley. Questioned by the reporter, to her astonishment Mary Whitehouse found herself declaring that she and Mrs Buckland intended to hold a public meeting—and were going to hire Birmingham's Town Hall which held 2,000 people. To this day, she remains amazed and bewildered at her own temerity.

In the event, however, everything transpired beyond their wildest hopes. The announcement in the Birmingham paper of the campaign to 'clean up' TV—MOTHERS CAMPAIGN FOR HIGHER TV MORALS ran the headline—was taken up by Fleet Street and within two days had drawn a response in the form of encouraging letters. During one day alone, 322 letters were delivered to Postman's Piece, Claverley. On the whole, with the exception of a group called 'steelworkers', the letters were from what the class-conscious Left Wing would categorize as 'middle-class': policemen, teachers, doctors, office workers, MPs, councillors. A great number were from men who had been in the services during the war and thought Britain was going to the dogs. Support for the campaign also came from the Chief Constable of Lincolnshire, Mr John Barnett. Many Chief Constables and local Watch Committees throughout the country, it seemed, faced with a terrifying increase in crime, took the view that BBC drama was partly responsible for a general loosening of the moral code.

As the campaign gained impetus, there is no doubt that a sizeable proportion of the population and of public opinion swung behind the leadership of Mrs Whitehouse and Mrs Buckland. From one viewpoint, much of the support was predictable: the Left claimed that every reactionary in the land had crawled out from beneath the stones. Prominent clergymen spoke in favour; the Catholic Teachers' Association and Catholic Women's League, the Scottish Housewives Association, the Free Evangelical Churches and the Free Church of Scotland—all

quite disparate groups—announced support and asked for
copies of the Manifesto. Signatures were to grow within two
years to almost a half-million. The critics of Mrs Whitehouse
and her movement have often dismissed her and her followers as
'non-intellectual' and 'unimaginative'. To this charge she had
replied that the signatories included a large number of professional people with university degrees; but even if the charge
were true, did not non-intellectual and unimaginative people
have as much right to have their views and opinions expressed as
any other group in Britain?

As she and her campaign gained momentum and even,
perhaps, influence, critics such as Roy Shaw, Head of the
Department of Extra-Mural studies at Keele University,
questioning the sources of her funds, claimed that it was sponsored by Moral Rearmament. Mary Whitehouse has categori-
cally denied this and, while admitting that both she and Norah
Buckland were members of that movement, says firmly that
only a few members of National VALA are also members of
Moral Rearmament and she estimates that MRA members have
contributed an insignificant amount of all moneys received.
She insists that great care has been taken to exclude controversial organisations or bodies trying to cash in on her campaign
for commercial reasons and as an example she quotes the fact
that before her great meeting at the Birmingham Town Hall, a
number of bodies whom she will not identify offered to sponsor
the meeting in exchange for the names and addresses of all who
had signed the Manifesto. Many people refuse to accept Mrs
Whitehouse's rebuttal of these charges and persist in the belief
that she is backed, if not by the CIA, at least by MRA; but I
find it difficult to believe she is speaking anything other than the
truth, given the sincerity of the woman, her genuine dedication
to her cause, the simplicity of her life, her obvious lack of
interest in material self-advancement plus the disgrace, humiliation and total destruction of her cause that would result if a
substantial link with any such organisation could be established.

She insists that her campaign has been kept alive solely by subscriptions to VALA and with the aid of voluntary donations. She cites the case of the old-age pensioner who sent her £1 in the first week of the campaign; the old Welsh lady who knitted over 90 dish-cloths to raise funds; the Sussex housewives who held a Bring-and-Buy sale; the collections raised at churches and meetings. In the early days, when Mary and Ernest were paying for the printing bills, there was a moment when they had only £6 left in the bank. Fortunately out of the blue arrived a cheque for £100 from somebody they had never heard of, with good wishes for their efforts.

The charge of unfairness, of special prejudice, has also been levelled at Mary Whitehouse because the main target of her criticisms has been the BBC, suggesting that she has soft-pedalled her approach to the Independent Television companies; or that they have, in some way, managed to get round her. She is conscious of these views and considers them as naive as they are inaccurate. What particularly sparked off her campaign and her career as a moral crusader was the output of two departments of the BBC: drama and current affairs programmes like *Meeting Point* which gave an undisputed platform to the protagonists of the Humanist and New Morality schools.

She does admit that the Independent Television Authority representatives showed a willingness to listen and to answer her points which was all she and her supporters have ever asked for. This contrasted with the behaviour of the BBC which seemed to think her an unmitigated nuisance who, if ignored, would simply go away. Sir Hugh Greene seems to have misjudged her indomitability and stamina, as well as the right degree of response to accord to the views or protests of a particular section of the public. It is obviously difficult for any directorate in the field of public communications to distinguish between a crank and a valid objector; so they naturally tend to rely on the channelled objections of pressure groups.

Nor was the situation as straightforward as Mrs Whitehouse

might want us to believe. The BBC had an austere image as 'Aunty', inherited from Lord Reith's own stern Scottish puritanism which he had imposed when he was Director-General. We often forget, for example, just how dreary Sunday radio broadcasts were in Britain back in the twenties and thirties; and this tradition greatly influenced television programmes in the fifties. Whatever the objections to Sir Hugh Greene's handling of affairs during his term of office, there can be no arguing that a gust of fresh air was badly needed—and in providing it, Greene performed a signal service. Nor, in parting from Mrs Whitehouse's ideal of a Christian broadcasting service (that is one based on the Judæo-Christian moral code) was Greene pursuing unacceptably radical views.

Neither the present Chairman of the BBC, Sir Michael Swann, nor the present Director-General, Sir Charles Curran, can be accused of being revolutionaries yet Curran himself has clarified the BBC's position with regards to its moral responsibilities. Speaking at Edinburgh in 1971, he declared, 'the first thing I must say is that we do not understand by the phrase "moral responsibility" an obligation to preach a particular form of conduct. It is not our job to adopt a particular morality and then to try to persuade everybody else to follow it. We are not, in our public roles, Christian, Muslim, Buddhist or Atheist. We are there to present—not to preach—these views of morality in so far as they are relevant to the society which we are addressing. It would clearly be misguided for us to preach the morality of the Koran to the British people. I think it might be reasonable further to suggest today that in what is in many ways a post-Christian era we are not in a position as an institution directly to commit ourselves to preaching Christianity. It is nevertheless a fact that the traditions of the country were formed in a Christian world and that its literature, past and present, its criteria of public conduct, and its public symbolic activities all reflect that fact. What we present of that literature, that conduct and those activities on the air is therefore bound to present a Christian face. To that extent our message is and must be Christian.'

'Right then, go to it!' would be Mrs Whitehouse's response. To Sir Charles, however, the issue is not so simple—nor is the demand for a Broadcasting Council, rather along the lines of the Press Council but hopefully with considerably more powers. 'It seems to me an inescapable necessity that, since our power as broadcasters is monopolistic, or quasi-monopolistic, we must see that we exercise it in a neutral fashion, giving opportunity for many views to be presented in as effective a way as we can achieve. But we are not, in the last resort, a moral weapon. We are a means of conveying messages which may be moral, according to the criteria which each of us in the audience applies.

'Perhaps it might help towards an understanding of the underlying difficulty if I were to suggest the problems which would arise if the BBC were to accept a specific responsibility for promoting a particular morality. Either some individual with final editorial authority would have to choose what course that would be, or the Board would have to reach some collective conclusion as to what was the acceptable morality which should represent the BBC's standpoint. As to the first possibility, I need only mention that I am myself a Roman Catholic for it to become self-evident that an arrangement whereby the moral course of the BBC was determined by the Director-General would be unacceptable to many. The same could be said if the Chairman were to be an adherent of a faith outside the latitudinarian Protestant tradition. And as for the second course— that there should be some kind of collective identification of the public morality to be promoted—I am bound to say that the pluralistic society in which we find ourselves has, throughout my eight-year acquaintance with the Board, been equally reflected among those who were its members. I cannot see that they would ever have agreed on which morality should be espoused by the BBC. Nor do I know by what authority they would commit themselves to such a morality even if they were able collectively to agree on one. That, it seems to me, is the great weakness in the argument put forward some time ago in the columns of *The Times*, where it was suggested that a Broadcasting Council . . . might be able . . . "to establish and apply generally acceptable notions of decency!" It is no business of people chosen to protect the public interest to dictate to the public a particular canon of public morality which many of their constituents might reject. That is why the Charter (of the BBC) is as imprecise as it is. And whenever I see reference in public statements to what is contained in the Charter by way of moral obligation, I know that the speaker cannot have read the document. It does no more than establish a corporate personality which then judges situations as best it can according to the consciences of the individuals who compose it . . . they are left to judge cases according to their best lights, as I have said, and in doing so, to take account of the general climate of opinion in which we live, assessing what is within the bounds of a widely tolerant amalgam of views and what, reluctantly and in extreme cases, must be held to exceed those limits. Our only stated obligation in the Charter, and therefore our central responsibility, is to serve the public. Now . . . we can obey the commands of the public . . . We can respond entirely to their dictation of what they want. That course would satisfy none of us in the BBC. But it is also possible to serve intelligently. By that I mean that we can detect in the ebb and flow of public opinion those things for which there is some demand, though not necessarily an overwhelming demand, and we can seek to meet the widest range of those demands. That seems to me to be the responsible path.'

Today there is a great deal in all this with which Mrs Whitehouse and the body of opinion which supports her would agree. Mrs Whitehouse has never demanded that the BBC should 'preach' Christianity. She would, perhaps, *like* it to—but that is not what is at issue. It is only when the Corporation has permitted contributors to promote an anti-Christian line or an anti-democratic line that she has felt it necessary to protest. Nor is it her argument that the anti-Christian or anti-democratic viewpoint should be banned. No, it should be rebutted, confronted, balanced in turn by its antithesis. On the other hand, she would forbid pornography completely. It would not be satisfactory to balance it by *not* showing pornography in turn as some have argued.

She sees the problems and difficulties rather more clearly nowadays, understanding 'the wheels within wheels' which operate a public corporation, appreciating the subtleties more easily. But people who see only the difficulties rarely get things done. It is those who are impelled by a clear and direct purpose who, in the last analysis, tend to move the world.

On May 5, 1964, Mrs Whitehouse, aided nobly by her friend Norah Buckland, put in her first little shove. She had approached the matter tentatively and with some trepidation—but whatever else could be said about the results, they were at least far from being tentative.

CHAPTER SIX

The Fight Continues

In a sense it was pure amateur night. The following morning *The Times* correspondent, commenting on 'the flimsy organisation', emphasised that it had 'no committee members, no officers and no hard plans for the future, except for the hope that the people at this meeting will go out and spread the word in other parts of the country'. It was a fair description of the 'organisation' that was first christened the Clean-Up TV Campaign and then developed into the National Viewers' and Listeners' Association claiming to have something in the region of 31,000 subscribing members.

The two ladies who had sparked off the idea had spent several uneasy weeks beforehand wondering how they were going to fill an enormous hall. They could only afford one large poster advertising the meeting outside Birmingham Town Hall and had to content themselves, in general, with writing to people who had declared support, enclosing tickets and leaflets and asking them to bring along their friends. Rushing home from school to the cottage at Claverley that afternoon, Mary Whitehouse was only slightly encouraged by the receipt of a telegram from the Archbishop of Canterbury expressing 'interest' and one from the Archbishop of York expressing 'support'. In Birmingham itself, her hopes rose slightly at the sight of a BBC television crew waiting for permission to televise the meeting.

Mary Whitehouse had never expected to be treated with kid gloves by the BBC but, as she tells the story, its representatives asked permission to use a 'silent camera' only—that is, one which would not record the speeches (or interruptions!) and they also promised not to interview anyone.

No fewer than thirty-seven coachloads of people had come from all over the country to help fill the giant hall. But from the outset, it was clear that 'wreckers' had been planted at strategic spots; and it was upon these spots that the BBC cameras— could it have been sheer coincidence?—mainly focussed.

When Mary Whitehouse, gathering strength and courage to face a tremendous ordeal—she had neither the experience nor technique to approach her task with equanimity—rose to take the microphone from Councillor Pepper, who was chairing the meeting, 'a bearded young tough' strode across the platform and attempted to pre-empt the instrument. As though at a given signal, hecklers arose in the body of the hall and for a few moments there was uproar. Ernest Whitehouse and his two sons dealt with the man who was trying to seize the microphone but from the hecklers in the body of the hall and from some of the 300 people sitting banked up behind the platform came the chant of 'We want sex' repeated over and over again. BBC spotlights were turned on the interrupters and the TV technicians were seen scurrying around the hall, trailing microphones (despite their promises), to make the most of the pandemonium. One BBC technician was heard to remark 'We can dish this lot!' Some of the younger members of the audience, however, struck back and ruined the 'fun' by turning out the spotlights. The rout of the enemy was completed when a row of Catholic nuns helped to drown out the hecklers by stamping loudly with their thick shoes. To this day, Mary Whitehouse remains convinced that the uproar was a completely put-up job intended for the benefit of the cameramen, a view reinforced when later that evening, BBC news, in transmitting their 'report' showed only the incidents with the hecklers.

Besides this confrontation with the hecklers and the media, the important inaugural meeting which led to the founding of the Clean-Up TV Campaign was to run into other problems.

There were those also at the meeting, however, who remain highly critical of the way it was conducted and of the kind of people who formed the majority of the audience. In general, this criticism seems to centre round the attitude adopted towards another interrupter—David Turner, the writer whose play *Trevor* was castigated from the platform by a group of local grammar school girls. Turner's play had been already the subject of savage criticism from the press—to such an extent, indeed, that he had been allowed to reply on radio. Turner himself now came forward and handed up a note to Councillor Pepper asking for permission to speak in his own defence. The request was refused. Mrs Whitehouse's answer to those who have criticised the 'silencing' of Turner is that the schedule of speakers was already 'pretty tight' (and the hecklers had probably made things worse) and that Turner had been already allowed to broadcast his defence to the country at large.

The meeting was a general success from Mary Whitehouse's viewpoint. *The Times*, though it qualified its comments by agreeing that 'there are those who will find it easy enough to laugh at the women who were here tonight', pointed out that many of the speakers 'had experience as teachers and social workers who were seriously concerned with social questions'. She was rather taken aback therefore when neither the Chairman of the BBC, Lord Normanbrook, nor Sir Hugh Greene would receive a deputation. It was not in fact until Lord Hill became chairman in September 1967 that she was formally received at Broadcasting House. She already knew Lord Hill, of course, as he had asked her to lunch when he was chairman of the ITA.

For Mary Whitehouse that meeting in Birmingham was the start, if rather a belated one, of her real career in life; a career which has now become the very *raison d'être* of her existence. To her astonishment, she became a magnet which drew together all the strands of discontent at BBC ideas of what was seemly for home viewing. Many felt that material that would have been then thought pretty 'hot' either for exhibition on stage or on the big screen was considered suitable for dissemination to a captive family circle. As much as anything else, their resentment was that there was no real escape from such material. With stage or cinema one had to be at least compulsively and morbidly interested before being drawn to watch. For millions throughout the country, however, it required a positive effort to switch off a TV set and sit and stare at a blank wall for most of an evening. As Sir Hugh Greene himself declared in an address given at the Alfred I. Dupont Awards Foundation dinner in Washington in March, 1962, on the subject of broadcasting freedom: 'How little in fact the ratings tell us. They tell us simply how many people watch a particular programme. They tell us nothing about the people themselves: who they are, why they watch; or how they enjoyed what they watched. Yet I should have thought that "why they watched" and "how much they enjoyed what they watched" were vital pieces of information in the planning of a responsible broadcasting service? Did they watch because they actually wanted to or merely because they were too apathetic to switch off? Did they actively enjoy the programme or did they merely tolerate it—a means of killing time for those who like time dead, as Rose Macaulay put it? . . . . The very simplicity of the concept of "giving the public what it wants"— and its too frequent use by those whose professional skill is cajolery of the simple-minded—should make us suspicious. . . .'

And violence? Although specifically referring to the American television makers' enormous output of material deeply bedded in crime—Westerns and crime and adventure stories—he added, 'Much more serious must be the ultimately corrupting effect of constantly seeing violence used, not only by criminals but by the upholders of what should be law and order. The shoddiest of all the shoddy arguments used to justify this is that such films are educational because, forsooth, they show the triumph of right over wrong.'

Yet as Mary Whitehouse has been quick to point out, the

BBC's policy during Sir Hugh's regime was scarcely one of eschewing violence. For example, the Corporation's second channel had been launched with an appropriate dedicatory service in, of all places, Westminster Abbey just prior to Mary's big meeting in Birmingham. Yet in its pursuit of 'powerful, real adult viewing—but with a purpose', the early days on the channel showed a man being branded with an iron, the desecration of a church by revolutionaries and the rape of a girl upon a Catholic altar. By the time Ken Taylor's trilogy, *The Seekers*, had run its course, viewers had been subjected to the sight of a bayoneting, a crushing under a jackboot, a beard set on fire, a suicide, a rape, a flogging and six brandings with an iron. The Americans, at least, made small excuse that the violence they portrayed was other than to make money and could thus be clearly seen to be wrong headed and perverted.

Undeterred by the refusal of senior BBC personnel to take her meeting or her campaign seriously, Mary Whitehouse, once a chronic invalid, set about fanning the fires of discontent with all the zeal and energy of a Marxist shop steward. From the outset she had no real operational plan, no long-term strategy, there was even very little discussion of tactics. To begin with, everything was rather impromptu and only time would lend a pattern to her personal activities. In the first year of the campaign, however, she addressed over a hundred meetings and travelled thousands of miles, all over Britain; read something like 18,000 letters from supporters and met approximately 15,000 people. The expenditure of energy was prodigious; one day in Birmingham, the next in Stoke, the next in London, the next in Mansfield. It was a punishing schedule and an amazing performance by a woman who almost had to change her personality to endure the ordeal of public speaking and of being in the public limelight.

It is tempting, perhaps, to dismiss Mary Whitehouse as a woman who thrust her way forward under the momentum of crankish ideas. Yet her success appears incredible—and indeed, could not have been possible—had she not been widely supported. Agreeing that the core of her support has been from those fully committed to Christianity, she insists that from the beginning much came from many who practised no religion at all. The National Viewers' and Listeners' Association now has 31,000 members and when it is criticised for being unrepresentative of anything but a tiny minority Mary gives comparative figures for other organisations: for all the prominence Humanist opinions are given on television, she points out, the total membership of the British Humanist society is only 2,000; that of the National Council for Civil Liberties, a mere 6,000. Even the number of paid-up members of the Labour party is only in the region of 300,000. Her 31,000 members, she claims, represent only the tip of an iceberg. Mrs Whitehouse says that she has the block support of organisations representing three million people.

'I talk to every kind of audience up and down the country and I've absolutely no doubt that the majority of people support what we do. At all my meetings, I find that whatever the enthusiasm shown, however, only an infinitesimal number actually join VALA. *But their support is there.* I've no doubt in my own mind that we've got widespread support throughout the whole country and among all classes. A lot of people are, perhaps, not prepared either to subscribe or actively support us—but they're jolly glad we exist, that we're there. I've never made membership a key thing anyway. Time and again I've travelled hundreds of miles to address a meeting and have had a marvellous audience, full of enthusiasm and when I've come away I've realised that I never even mentioned anyone joining the Association. Things have got a little better since Ernest began to help me full time—but the truth is that for me, putting across the message has been the important thing. The message?—that in a democracy everyone has a right to have their voice heard. I think one of the most frightening aspects of the last ten years is the extent to which people want to try and silence us by exclusion. If we had not been so determined and committed, I believe their efforts would have paid off.

'To revert to the membership question—well, it doesn't take account of the block support we receive; by that, I mean the support of women's organisations whose own memberships run into thousands. For instance, one of the most recent groups to join us is the Association of Stage Schools which represents about 20,000 people—they joined because they are very worried at the kind of jobs some of their graduates are asked to take. I mean young actresses find they can't get work unless they agree to strip or do a nude scene. It's been the extent, the range of support and the depth of it that's always made me realise that I could never stop, never give up—even though I've been often sorely tempted to.'

'She no longer cries these days as she once did,' says her youngest son. 'In the beginning she found the attacks quite harrowing, you know, and if her campaign has changed her, it has been only to make her more hardened to other people's attacks. Nowadays, in fact, the attacks run off her as off a duck's back. But it wasn't always like that—and she used to cry when things got on top of her.'

What kind of woman was this anyway—this woman who could rise from obscurity when the greater part of her life's course was run to become a household word in Britain?

'If somebody had said to me back in 1963 that my mother would have done what she has managed to do, I'd have said, "You must be joking" ' replies her son Christopher. 'She was certainly the sort of woman capable of getting up some kind of a petition, perhaps, but none of us ever dreamed she could go beyond that.' And she had her feminine frailties, of course. For instance, she still has an almost complete blind spot about motor-cars, often forgetting that they need petrol, water and oil before they will function properly. For years she was convinced that it was the fan under the bonnet that actually pulled the car along—more or less like the propeller of an aeroplane. Even now, she will often drive out of the gate of Triangle Farm heading for Cambridge, and instead drive off towards Glasgow.

What particular qualities did she possess? Well, nothing outstanding really. She is not particularly well-read: years ago she might have read Maugham, Priestley and Wells. She possesses an even temper and is never either depressive or euphoric. She no longer needs to pluck up courage to speak in public—in this respect her son considers that she obviously feels a little like St Joan girding on her armour. 'She has her banner—and is prepared to wave it and if people don't like it, well, that's too bad.'

To the criticism that she is arrogant—arrogant in trying to determine or influence what the British public shall or shall not see—her son readily understands that some people might consider her to be so because she is prepared to stand up and say what she thinks. 'But arrogance implies a sense of superiority—and I can truthfully say that my mother has never felt herself to be superior to anybody. It just isn't her way—it just isn't her method of looking at things. Nor is she really a crank. She really is just an ordinary housewife.

'The campaign *has* caused her much personal agony from time to time, but it would be wrong to think of her as essentially a shy person—shy in the sense of being timid, that is. She was never an outgoing, extrovert sort of person—and to that extent the campaign has changed her. Nowadays she is more self-assured, more confident—but that is because she has no doubt about what she is doing, is absolutely certain that what she is doing is right.'

What her son remembers with gratitude is that both Mary and Ernest provided him and his brothers with 'a very happy home—it was a place where there was never any shortage of love'. There was discipline, though. 'When I did something wrong, they'd say, "You're spoilt" and I'd answer back impertinently, "Well, who spoilt me, then?"—which would earn me a slap or a wallop as the occasion demanded. Actually, there was hardly any physical punishment. Our parents set the boundaries of behaviour and any time we overstepped those, we were chastised usually by being sent to bed early or deprived of

other privileges. The best thing about both mother and father—
and father *could* be very stern—was that they were always consistent in their attitude, so that you always knew where you
stood. I think we always appreciated the fact that they were
both even-tempered people—that we were not subjected to
quite arbitrary changes of mood which would totally disorientate
us.'

The details of the portrait are quickly etched in, then. A
woman who is just sufficiently house-proud to be feminine and
very human; an art-teacher who does not particularly like
abstracts. A husband who loves classical music and who had a
rather unbending attitude towards the working man. A couple
who together like the quiet beauties of life—a walk in the
countryside, perhaps, above all. Whose idea of a holiday is not
a Spanish beach but a walk in Italy, spying out old medieval
fortress towns built on hilltops. A couple unbendingly driven and
quietly inspired by their faith.

Many of her friends and well-wishers in both television and
Fleet Street tend to see Mary Whitehouse as rather a cut above
most of her supporters. They describe her as a 'more impressive
figure' without being more precise; they seem to mean that most
of her followers have retained a naivety with which contact and
battle with her opponents have now rid Mary. Yet there are
supporters who seem to me quite impressive like Mrs Polly
Bennett, for example, who runs the Essex branch of VALA.

'We had to bring up our three boys during that difficult
period during the sixties when things were changing so rapidly,'
explains Polly. 'I used to get terribly concerned when I walked
into the sitting room where the boys were watching television
and saw the kind of stuff that was being put out. I used to feel
compelled to walk across and either switch the set off or turn to
the other channel. I found it hard to believe that the BBC, which
we had all learned to love and admire, had become an insidious
thing attacking our very homes. England, after all, is a country
where ordinary people are busy about their ordinary jobs, dig-

ging their ordinary gardens and painting their ordinary houses. It's not in a state of revolution. Go to any ordinary town, made up of little people in little streets—go to towns like Coventry or Norwich, where people have their little TV sets but don't want to hear their children having to listen to bloodies and four-letter words and all the other sort of things that are put out. I sometimes feel that people in the BBC and Fleet Street are living in a little world of their own which has nothing to do with the rest of the country.'

It was in this mood then that Polly Bennett and her husband first attended one of VALA's conventions. 'We came away absolutely enthused. We found Mary Whitehouse a fantastic character; and with it, human. We had met many famous people during our lives but Mary thoroughly impressed us. Her integrity, her single-mindedness, her courage, the fact that she was never without a sense of humour. I think the reason she arouses so much opposition is that she inevitably hits the nail right on the head. But she's really a very sensitive person. Even now she is vulnerable—despite all she's seen, and felt.'

'She has one other attribute worth noting,' insists Bill Deedes. 'It is not singular—but I have noticed it in my life as a member of Parliament—this, I may say, doesn't endear her to me or my friends. Nonetheless, it ought to be mentioned. She is never in the least inhibited at any hour of the day or night in ringing you up, asking you for what she wants and asking directly and putting you to some inconvenience. The world really is divided into rather cautious, nervous people who would hesitate to ring up friends or acquaintances and demand certain things off them on the telephone and those who, I suspect, have got rather further than most of us, who never hesitate. I've had constituents, most of them rather successful, who have never hesitated to ring up me or my wife at any hour of the clock and ask for what they want. My mother used to say: "Never use the telephone because you don't give the person at the other end a chance to refuse—always put it in writing." Mary's not like that. If she wants something, she lifts the telephone. It's a technique of getting what you want—which I've noticed in other successful people besides Mary Whitehouse. She's extremely direct—you don't get a letter saying "I wonder if you might be free or available to do this or that". She rings up and starts, "Bill, there's something I want you to do for me." You're immediately put in the position of having to refuse or say yes—and one's inclined to say yes. I regard this as one of her secret weapons. She's a masterful user of the telephone.'

Mary Whitehouse and Norah Buckland never hesitated in going for the top. With the aid of two MPs who gave them and their campaign every support, James Dance and Jasper More, they sent a deputation to Reginald Bevins, the Postmaster-General and minister responsible for broadcasting. This action lent a dignity to what was still an *ad hoc* organisation which, it could be argued, was not very representative. Kenneth Adam, then Controller of BBC TV, in a letter to the Church of England Newspaper describing her as 'offensive and ignorant', declared that delegates representing ten million women affiliated to official or national women's organisations had attended a meeting at TV Centre and had shown very different opinions from those expressed by Mrs Whitehouse. Sir Hugh Greene himself wrote a letter to an MP declaring that 'none (of the delegates at the meeting) had any sympathy with the criticisms of the Birmingham women'. Mary Whitehouse admits that these two letters constituted a severe psychological setback to her campaign. Even today Polly Bennett admits that many women's organisations are reluctant to have anything to do with Mary 'mainly because of the distorted image given by TV and the press'. But when her supporters in the organisations represented at the BBC meeting investigated what had been actually discussed, they learned that both Adam's and Greene's statements appeared to be at variance with the facts. Questions such as 'sadistic' displays of violence, the 'casual' treatment of sex and other 'exploitation of sexual behaviour' *had* been raised—the very issues on which Mary Whitehouse herself had taken a stand.

Yet despite BBC efforts to belittle Mrs Whitehouse, support continued to grow. Regular meetings of the *ad hoc* committee were held, at one of which it was suggested she should become the official spokesman for the organisation. A treasurer was also appointed and a part-time typist, the only paid member of the group, was engaged. Every four to six weeks, a newsletter went out to almost 7,000 supporters, stamped and dispatched by volunteers working in different parts of Birmingham. One of her sons even modified his bedroom so that it could serve as official headquarters of the movement.

All this time, Mary Whitehouse went on teaching at Madeley Secondary School, while dealing with three hundred letters almost every evening after her day's work and travelling all over the place to address meetings. Once, she drove straight from school to address a meeting in the Liverpool Philharmonic Hall and then back as far as Chester where she slept the night. A 6.30 a.m. rise saw her back again in school in good time but during the day Ernest telephoned to tell her that a long-awaited meeting with a group of MPs had been scheduled for London that evening. He picked her up outside the school in the afternoon, drove her the 120 miles to London and then back to Wolverhampton the following morning after a brief night's sleep. It was obvious that it was no longer possible to continue doing both jobs. It says much for Mary Whitehouse's courage and determination that she decided to give up a salary of £1,500 a year (at 1965 values) and useful pension rights in order to continue her campaign which, so far as she could then foresee, was unlikely to yield her any pecuniary advantage. She was aware by this time that her campaign was likely to produce a backlash from quite unexpected quarters. She had been offered the post of Senior Mistress, Lower School, in a new comprehensive to be formed from Madeley Secondary Modern and the local grammar school—but a delay occurred in ratifying her appointment.

Indeed, only the personal intervention of the new Headmaster finally secured her appointment. Although she still went ahead with her resignation, he agreed to keep the job open for some time. She admits that because of the campaign of villification that greeted her, she was often near the point of resuming her teaching career.

Typical of the kind of calumny she had to face was Ned Sherrin's rather contemptuous remark in an interview with the *Daily Mail* about the forthcoming 'Not So Much a Programme, More a Way of Life'. Then at the height of his fame and success, the young Sherrin said 'I think we've dulled people's capacity for shock. I'm told one woman has already given up her job so she can monitor the programme and be ready to protest. What puzzles me is—what sort of a job was she doing that kept her busy at the hour of the night when we're on the air? I suppose she must have been on the streets.' After consulting Quintin Hogg (Lord Hailsham) in his professional capacity as a Q.C. Mary Whitehouse won 'sincere apologies' along with £500 damages and legal costs in the High Court.

As Mary Whitehouse sees it, the counter-attacks on her Clean-Up TV campaign consisted of a deliberate smear—that she and her supporters were out to 'censor' TV. She sees Sir Hugh Greene as leading the attack and quotes an article he wrote for the *Listener* on June 17, 1965, which began 'These attempts at censorship came not merely from the old Guardians. . . . The attempts at censorship come nowadays from groups—(Professor Richard) Hoggart calls them "the new populists"—who . . . claim to speak for "ordinary decent people". Sir Hugh, of course, had considerable support for his attitude, particularly, she notes, from among Methodist church leaders and Anglican supporters of the New Morality. It is Mary Whitehouse's case, of course, that she has never demanded censorship—but in the beginning it would appear that there can be little doubt that that is what she intended; and most certainly it was what the vast mass of her supporters intended. As the campaign gathered pace and force, however, as the public argument grew, as she found herself becoming more and more knowledgeable of the facts of life behind the TV cameras, so her own arguments became more sophisticated, more adult—and very much more significant.

In the beginning, however, there were two spheres of activity where she felt BBC TV desperately needed cleaning up—in the area of discussion programmes and, so far as 'dirt and filth' were concerned, principally in the field of drama. She is on pretty firm ground when she argues that she felt that little but the 'trendy' point of view was being allowed in BBC television discussions; in the field of drama, however, her demands could have been met only by some form of censorship. A decade later, her arguments would be those of a veteran and by that time people who had worked inside TV would have seen the validity of her viewpoint.

In a paper entitled *Television and the Consumer* which she read at a symposium on the 'Role and Management of Telecommunications in a Democratic Society' at Munich in June, 1974, she was able to declare, 'They (the professional broadcasters) see their freedom of expression at risk. But television is a unique medium in that it is projected into the home and it is a fact that large quantities of children are still watching during so-called "adult" viewing time. . . . The freedom of the professional has to be balanced against the right of the individual to maintain certain standards within his own home, to sit and view without having to accept gratuitous indecency and foul language as an integral part of the evening's entertainment. . . . Television . . . must be the subject of democratic control and the challenge to us is to seek ways in which this may be implemented without denying either of the basic freedoms referred to. The challenge, in essence, is to create a situation in which conviction and tolerance can co-exist.

'There are two problems, the one posed by a mass-viewing public . . . and the other by the possessive attitude of producers and playwrights who genuinely seem to believe that broadcast-

ing belongs to them and have a great impatience, even intolerance, of critics who appear to them to be illiberal and unedu-
cated. The need for a meeting of minds has never been so
imperative. . . . The truth is that some of those who write and
produce live in too small a world. They have . . . failed to
grasp the very nature of the medium in which they work. . . .
The television studio and its contents are only a small part of
their equipment. They will manipulate not only the cameras but
hearts and minds as well. . . . We are faced with a great divide
—the gap between those who produce and those who receive
programmes. That the gap is polluted by a great deal of mis-
understanding, resentment, even bitterness, cannot be doubted.
. . . The only acceptable alternative to dictatorship either
from within or without the medium is an informed and involved
populace. Democracy must be made to work within broadcasting as elsewhere. The responsibility must be accepted as "ours"
rather than "theirs".'

In fact, it is easy, perhaps, to detect a certain slight, if under-
standable, degree of hypocrisy in these words. The hypocrisy
may be considered defensible, however, in that it was merely a
form of diplomatic language. Mary Whitehouse knew as well as
anybody that the men whom she was exhorting to remember
that they manipulated hearts and minds as well as TV cameras
were only too well aware of this fact already; she knew that the
real battle was between those who held one view of what society
in Britain should be like and others who considered that the
proposed changes in that society—a tolerance to violence, to explicit sexual material, to the use of obscene and blasphemous
language, to explicit revolutionary or anti-authoritarian views,
were a deliberate attempt to subvert and destroy the delicate
balance that make a stable democratic society. The problem was
not so much 'censorship', as identifying those who directly or
indirectly controlled television production in the BBC. What
kind of people were they?

Anthony Jay, a former BBC executive, and later associated

with David Frost, identified part of the problem when he said that the trouble with the BBC was that it was loaded with 'people whose social, political and moral assumptions are opposed to the majority of the country and there is a kind of consensus among them on a variety of topics—which are at best partisan opinions and at worst the opinions of a small educated middle-class left-wing minority.'

In his Fleming Memorial Lecture of 1973, Dennis Forman, joint Managing Director of Granada TV, pointed out that a rather similar situation also existed in parts of ITV. He talked of 'the sense of ownership of the means of creation enjoyed by TV executives' and of groups within TV journalism which form their 'own ethnic identity and canons of journalism'. Marsland Gander, then *Daily Telegraph* TV critic, suggested that TV was 'a cosy secret society'. As Mrs Whitehouse adds, 'What makes this particular problem more intractable is that it is self-perpetuating. Like breeds like. New recruits are attracted—and chosen—because they hold similar views, values and attitudes to those already established within the broadcasting profession, while those who hold to more traditional—or less radical—life styles tend to find the atmosphere within the medium uncongenial and uncompromising.'

The 'counter-attack', as she calls it, taught Mary Whitehouse much about the manipulations of British society that, until she began her campaign, she had only vaguely suspected. The only criticism that might be reasonably levelled at her at this point is that her view was a narrow one that took no account of that society's complex ramifications—levels of behaviour and environment and experience that quite clearly lay beyond her experience. But that, as she points out hastily today, was all a long time ago.

CHAPTER SEVEN

An Amateur Against Experts

Then there was TRACK (Television and Radio Committee) formed in 1965. According to the *Humanist News*, this organisation sprang from the initiatives of five well-known TV playwrights—among them Troy Kennedy Martin of *Z Car* fame, Clive Exton (whose work is still applauded by the critics) and David Mercer—whom I personally once heard urge the notion that rape should be performed twice nightly on a West End stage. The *Guardian* newspaper, for one, had no doubt that TRACK was formed to counteract Mary Whitehouse. The Humanist Association immediately offered its help, which was accepted 'without prejudice'. TRACK's headquarters, according to Mary Whitehouse, were at 13 Prince of Wales Terrace, which, possibly by coincidence, is also the address of various radical organisations like the Union of Democratic Control—along with such organisations as the Euthanasia Society, the Progressive League, the Socialist Medical Association and the Ethical Union.

And then there was the COSMO group founded by a Harlow councillor called Mrs Avril Fox who in a staged discussion with Mrs Whitehouse in a Fleet Street newspaper office declared that she would have no objection to allowing her children to view sexual intercourse on TV or even view an act of murder—in close up. Although these people could be considered a lunatic fringe, millions throughout the country took the view that Mary herself represented another extreme. She thinks of the allegation that her campaign was backed by Moral Rearmament as a smear; but was it not to some extent justified? After all, both she and Norah Buckland had been long-term members of MRA.

Nonetheless, a group of 30 people met in the Grosvenor House hotel, Park Lane, early in 1965 to discuss forming a more substantial forum from which to influence television production than the mere emotional outcry of protest that the Clean-Up TV campaign represented. The Anglican Bishop of Hereford was there; a representative of the Catholic Archbishop of Westminster; six members of Parliament; a representative of the Methodist church; the Chief Constable of Lincoln and a representative of the Scottish Housewives' Association, and others. At this meeting the idea of a Viewers' and Listeners' Association was first mooted. Parents, they felt, should have a voice in what was televised and VALA would provide that opportunity.

'We do not see its overall function as one of censorship . . . Rather it would make available for those responsible for programmes highly specialised thinking on a much wider front than is at present at the disposal of producers,' declared Mrs Whitehouse ringingly. The Methodist representative was unconvinced and shortly afterwards severed all connection with the idea on the grounds of its 'negative approach'. Some time later, the Association adopted its present name, the National Viewers' and Listeners' Association.

The idea that the Association would censor TV material was carefully picked on by its opponents but, to be fair, if Mary Whitehouse ever entertained any such idea (apart from seeking to control material that could be viewed by children), she soon realised its futility. Her role was to point out new directions by picking on the shortcomings of the old. The sheer lack of subtlety about much of the material that she objected to rapidly established the fact that she had a valid point. She objected to the play *Up the Junction* principally because she felt it was propaganda for the Abortion Law Reform Bill, then before Parliament. At that, the balance could have been restored, she argued, had medical men who took the opposite view been allowed proportionate time to put their viewpoint. It was the *distortion* of human experience in Britain by television that she was really objecting to. A TV programme could make an opinion or viewpoint seem like the *only* truth.

The more those who detested Mary Whitehouse poured calumny upon her, the more she flourished. On June 3, 1965, the great Manifesto signed by 365,355 people, expressing concern about the 'low standards' of TV programmes, was presented to Parliament. In just over a year, Mary Whitehouse had earned herself a niche in British national life and, far from being stopped in her tracks, was to exercise a growing and still flourishing influence.

A week later, Mary Whitehouse found herself being lunched by members of the Independent Television Authority and invited to address them briefly by Lord Hill, then the Authority's chairman. When accused of being 'soft' on ITV, her invariable answer is that, from the outset, the ITA had adopted the policy of recognising her and her movement as a group, however much a minority, whose viewpoint was entitled to be heard and considered. Hill, of course, was a wily old bird who knew all about getting round people while both Normanbrook, a retired senior civil servant, and Greene had been insulated from direct contact with the ordinary public. It was an ivory-tower attitude which soon had VALA baying for Greene's blood. Brian Walden, a Labour MP who bitterly opposed Mrs Whitehouse's views, warned her that she was wasting her time attacking Sir Hugh personally: he *was* the Establishment. In Walden's view he had been 'responsible' for putting the Labour Government in power and there was absolutely no chance that the government would sack him. But in the end he went.

For Mary Whitehouse, an exciting new life had suddenly begun to open up. By any standards it was exhilarating: invitations to appear on German TV; hordes of newspaper feature writers descending on the cottage at Claverley; the constant ringing of the telephone; the fuss over *Up the Junction* (she indignantly refuted the suggestion that she had 'organised' the flood of protests that jammed the BBC switchboard); National VALA's first Press Conference, held in Fleet Street itself. There was also the darker side—the obscene phone calls; the need for a bodyguard to protect her when she addressed meetings; the detective who called to warn her that according to a London evening newspaper, two men were on their way from London to get her; the eventual need for police protection wherever she went.

Early in the new year, VALA organised a monitoring scheme of 1,000 programmes, carried out by 175 people, the idea being to assess the discernible trends in television and radio so far as was possible, even if in an unsophisticated and admittedly un-scientific way. On April 30, 1966, VALA held its first annual Convention in Birmingham, the main speaker being Bill Deedes. Deedes instantly made his own position clear. A journalist as well as a politician, he declared himself passionately against censorship 'which was not the safeguard of a civilised nation; it is a most ominous symptom of its ill-health'. It was because he abhorred 'censorship that I support this movement'. He realised that unless better means were devised to govern this explosive influence, television, then inevitably demand for control—'and political control at that'—would grow stronger. Deedes agreed that the BBC's 'present system of internal government' was in-adequate and perceived the urgent need for a 'right system' of government within television 'before the politicians are pushed into the act'.

The Convention was a triumph for Mrs Whitehouse and a vindication of much she had been arguing for. In fact, as she has rightly pointed out, hers was neither the first nor the only voice raised in protest against certain aspects of television output. Four years before she had started her campaign, the Pilkington Report had noted, 'There is no doubt that concern is widespread and acute. It cannot be dismissed as the unrepresentative opinion of well-meaning but over-anxious critics, still less as that of cranks. . . . The consideration that gave rise to this feeling was usually that . . . television portrayed too often a world in which the moral standards normally accepted in society were either ignored or flouted.'

Mrs Whitehouse was making out a persuasive case and even Hugh Greene was forced to take note. In the BBC's Handbook for 1966, there appeared an article dealing with the controversy and from this it was clear that even among religious bodies, there were those who at least tended to side with the BBC in upholding that it had 'a positive duty' to 'shock, disturb and anger'. The *Guardian* took the view that the BBC should not be asked to 'blur over the sharp edges of our discontents, of our religious questionings, of our frustrations in human relationships'. No wonder that Mary Whitehouse, in those early days, often sat down and cried. She was not asking that controversy should be stilled; she was arguing that only *one* side of the controversy was being allowed an airing and that too much of 'serious' TV output was concerned with the violent, sordid, hopeless and miserable aspects of life. By any objective standards, this was surely an *unbalanced* view of British society. Nor could it be fairly argued that the only people with the necessary gifts and talents to write successful plays were those who held left-wing views or were committed to social change. This would have meant that politics were paramount—a Stalinist view of the artist's role which few could any longer accept.

Much of the output of The Wednesday Play, an important BBC drama series, seemed dedicated to offensive, even subversive plays. One called *For the West* dealing with the Congo situation was described by Milton Shulman in the London *Evening Standard* as 'vicious, crude propaganda that one used to associate with the less edifying techniques of Goebbels'. Religious sensitivities were also ruthlessly trampled upon—*The Bachelors* was about Catholic priests who were allegedly practising homosexuals. Ted Willis (now a Labour peer), president of the Screenwriters' Guild, was forced to declare himself 'sick and tired' of plays where the whole action was about 'who sleeps with whom'. Whatever Sir Hugh Greene's philosophical reasons for allowing such plays, however much an articulate section of British society screamed against 'censorship', any fair-minded person who approached the subject objectively had to admit that not only had the Clean-Up TV people a point, but that their ideas struck a sympathetic chord among many who could by no means be classified as 'non-intellectual' or 'ignorant'. That a cumulative effect was being created was proved when Sydney Newman, head of BBC television drama, felt compelled to issue a memo to his producers warning them about the treatment of sex and religion, a warning repeated for the second time within twelve months when producers were told to exercise greater control over the use of violence, sex and bad language.

'Very charming people, running their own show, more or less' was how Reginald Bevins, Postmaster-General from 1959 to 1964, described the BBC managers after he had quit office. Bevins noted that despite Parliamentary questions and protests from the public, the BBC 'usually turns a blind eye' to opinions contrary to its own, 'not all of which come from cranks or bigots' and instances two or three occasions on which he informally spoke to the BBC about their material only to receive no reaction at all or simply 'an explaining-away' reply.

Few programme series have raised such a storm of controversy in Britain as Johnny Speight's *Till Death Us Do Part* which starred Warren Mitchell as Alf Garnett. What infuriated Mary Whitehouse and National VALA was not so much the outrageous opinions and viewpoints expressed by Alf Garnett, as the coarseness of the language he used. Both Dennis Main Wilson, the producer of the show, and Johnny Speight himself argue vehemently that neither swear words nor foul language have ever been used on the show. The word 'bloody', they argue, for all its grotesque use as an expletive, is not a swear word.

Johnny Speight and Dennis Main Wilson are proud of their working-class origins and everyone knows that there are house-

holds and environments all over Britain where strong language
is the rule rather than the exception. But the argument for
realism does not necessarily condone the use of the language of
Billingsgate on a mass-audience medium. Amid the welter of
'bloodies', 'bitches', 'moo-cows', 'gits' and 'coons', however,
many of the points Johnny Speight intended to make were lost.
A radical who was satirising the stupidity of racial prejudice,
Speight found the pathetic nature of Alf's character soon had
people's sympathy. Garnett's views were taken literally and few
grasped the irony. Many of the views expressed by characters in
the series were gratuitously offensive and purposeless; remarks
about the Virgin Mary being 'on the pill' or that the Bible is
'bloody rubbish' irritated certain sections of the community
without making the British public any more tolerant of the
Asian or black minorities within their midst. When God was
originally described in one script as being 'worse than Hitler',
even the BBC cut it out.

In America, Sir Hugh Greene was asked about the programme
and quizzed in particular about the offence it obviously gave to
many people. 'It only offends those one would wish to offend'
was his lofty if epigrammatic reply.

Mary Whitehouse had reacted predictably to the first flood
of foul language and blasphemy by pointing out that the programme as initially put out was bound to be seen by children.
The BBC put back transmission to peak viewing time. Protests
were drowned by the very popularity of the programme which
was certainly most comical. Johnny Speight rode out the storm
of protest raised by Mary Whitehouse pretty successfully until
he made some extravagant remarks on a radio programme. He
declared that the 'Clean-Up TV people' were 'hypocritically
concealing' their 'fascism under the cloak of a moral campaign'
and added that the implication was that they were racialists and
'like the killers of Christ'. Mary Whitehouse first attempted to
extract an apology from the BBC, writing directly to Lord
Normanbrook, then Chairman of the Corporation. She received

Constance Mary Hutcheson
aged 2 years 7 months.

Aged eight.

Her first job at Lichfield Road School,
Wednesfield, Wolverhampton, 1931

In Girl Guide Camp, 1932.

*Wedding day, 23 March 1940,
St Peter's Church, Chester.*

*Ernest with the three boys
(l to r Christopher, Paul, Richard)
on holiday at Llwyngyvie, 1951.*

*First anniversary of
Clean-Up TV Campaign,
Midland Hotel,
Birmingham, January
1965.
Ernest and Mary
Whitehouse, Mrs Norah
Buckland, Revd Basil
Buckland.*

SUNDAY MERCURY,
BIRMINGHAM

*Clean-Up TV Manifesto
with half a million
signatures ready for
presentation to Parliament
June 1965.*

Press Conference to launch National Viewers and Listeners Association, November 1965. Mary Whitehouse, James Dance MP, Dr Ernest Claxton (Assistant Secretary, BMA).

A Pleasant surprise for all. Mick Jagger with Mary Whitehouse on the David Frost show, 28 October 1968.

*With Malcolm Muggeridge at the National Festival of Light Rally
at Trafalgar Square, 23 September 1971.*

DAILY TELEGRAPH

Mrs Whitehouse meets Pope Paul VI, Castel Gondolfo, August 1971.

Mary Whitehouse with the Hon. Milton Morris, NSW Minister for Transport and the Young World Singers at the packed Sydney Town Hall Rally of the Australian Festival of Light, October 1971.

National VALA Award to 'Softly, Softly', 26 February 1975: (PC Dodds), Frank Windsor (Det. Chief-Superintendent Watt), Mary Whitehouse, Stanley Parr, Chief Constable Lancashire.

With Sir Keith Joseph at National VALA Convention February 1975.

Moment of victory. Press Conference after Mrs Enid Wistrich loses Greater London Council 'no film censorship' battle, 29 January 1975.

PRESS ASSOCIATION LTD

no satisfaction and it was only when the word 'fascist' was hurled at her during lecture visits to various universities in the succeeding weeks that she finally took an action for libel in the High Court and won a full apology with costs and some hundreds of pounds damages which she gave to National VALA.

Today Johnny Speight harbours no particular ill-feeling against Mary Whitehouse. When I asked him: 'What influence has she had on television?', he told me, 'I don't think she's had much'. Mary Whitehouse would contest that, pointing out that Sir John Eden, Minister of Posts and Telecommunications from 1972 to 1974 during the last Conservative Government, had written her regarding 'the need for some improvements in the standards observed in broadcasting' and that as a result of discussions with concerned groups such as her own, certain views had been passed on to the broadcasting authorities. 'This undoubtedly has led to a review of practices by the broadcasters, some evidence of which is seen in the revised code of conduct and the improved relationship between the advisory councils and the authorities. There is no doubt in my mind that there is a much greater awareness now than there was of the need to guard against excesses either of obscenity or violence in broadcasting,' Eden added.

Johnny Speight, of course, has never made any secret of where his political sympathies lie. 'I'm very much a political animal, certainly,' he told me. 'I think I'm a left-wing socialist. Some think I'm a neo-Nazi because I think Nietzsche one of the greatest philosophers that's ever been around; Hitler, of course, vulgarised him. I'm very much a Shavian, actually.

'I think we're really going forward all the time, even in this country. The lower class is moving forward. Certainly it's not articulating all its needs yet. But it's got to formulating its wants. What they want now is not what they need—and they need someone to tell them what they need, for often the things one needs are not what one wants. That box in the corner of the room encourages people to want things—but people are slowly beginning to realise that Daz is no whiter than Omo, that you can't tell the difference between one dog meat and another. At the moment the masses are simply demanding more—eventually they will demand more quality to life.

'So far as I'm concerned, if I attack this country—and I suppose I do—yet there's still no other country in the world I'd rather live in, simply because I love it. I think it's the Greece of the modern world. It's one of the few countries in the world where things get printed; great journalists still get their copy through. Oh, sure, I believe a lot of people subscribe to Mary Whitehouse—just as a lot subscribe to Alf Garnett. I wouldn't say she's been a really bad influence—but I couldn't agree either that she's been a good one. I sometimes feel that she's got through to some of the more chicken-hearted people in the BBC.

'I'm not against her in particular—but I believe that if she and all she stands for had their way, there would be no room for any improvement in this country at all. We'd become sterile. Art *can* be dangerous—it can bring in ideas that at the moment don't seem to be to our good, but they are still worth hearing. In dictatorial states, of course, they clamp down on all art. Because art offends the actual opinions of the day, it doesn't mean to say that these opinions are the right ones. Because the majority of the day believe in a certain opinion, doesn't necessarily mean that that is the right opinion, either. When Jesus Christ came around, the opinion of his day wasn't his—and what did they do, they crucified him. You must allow these ideas to come out into the open—once you start clamping down on them, you're fast becoming a sick society. You're frightened to face truths—you call them lies. Better to let things come out in the open and find out if it's a truth or lie about our society or yourself. The type of thing she does, I believe, would be to stop all that.

'As for this argument that TV has been taken over by Left Wing groups, I believe that's completely untrue. It's neither Left nor Right in my opinion but unfortunately in the very middle of the road—even the political programmes are middle of the road. They put out what they think the average half-wit will enjoy—and treat their audience with complete disrespect. The whole structure of politics is unfair—not fair to the average bloke who has too much trouble already trying to run his own life. And she seems to want democracy to be run by a committee —a self-appointed committee.

'She says, "don't use bad language on the show"—but I only use "bloodies" and to me that's not an offensive word. All right, I've used the word "cobblers" a few times, but I've never used "piss off" which gets into other shows. In fact, there's a lot more innuendo and smut in other shows and none of these are attacked. She's championing all that's worst in the medium by not attacking them—she appears to me to attack only the serious viewpoints about society. It's going back to the way things used to be in this country where you could say anything dirty you liked in a music hall turn but if you attempted to use the same language or express the same ideas in a serious play, the Lord Chamberlain immediately banned you.

'As for Alf Garnett—well I've written him as I saw him. To me there are prototypes of Alf all over the country; far too many of them in fact. And if I didn't use words like "blast" and "blow me" and so on, he wouldn't be a real character. And he *is* a real character. But what I set out to do was to show the idiocy of his ideas by bouncing them against other ideas, some of them, perhaps, equally extreme and absurd. That's the function of the artist—and that was what was so great about Hugh Greene; he believed in artists having as much freewheel as they could possibly gain for themselves; yet he remained the first to come down on anything we'd call purely vulgar or pornographic.'

Yet if Johnny Speight felt he were being battered and his freedom grossly interfered with by censorious groups, Mary Whitehouse was learning how easy it is to be made a fool of in public. After the publication of her book, *Cleaning up TV*, in 1967, she was invited to appear on Bernard Braden's programme on

ITV. The interview was filmed and although it lasted over two
hours, only 2½ minutes of actual screen time was devoted to
her. Braden courteously telephoned her beforehand and read
her over the script but warned her that there had been 'a great
deal of studio laughter'. In the event, when he asked her 'Do
you think BBC plays go too far?,' she got only as far as saying 'I
don't think they go far enough'—when the rest of her reply—
'because they fail to show that conflict between good and evil
which is the essence of good drama'—was drowned by the studio
laughter. It was yet another shattering experience for her, nor
were her feelings alleviated when VALA supporters rang up to
say that she appeared to stand for the very things they were
against. The Director-General of the ITA, Sir Robert Fraser,
sent her a copy of the script with an apology and when she saw
what had been actually planned by the Braden staff, she had to
agree that the presence of a studio audience can often wreck the
emphasis of any show. In a way it taught her to be more tolerant
of the difficulties experienced by even the most well-meaning
TV producers; also to realise how easy it is for manipulators to
distort the truth. She was advised that she should never again
agree to a filmed interview, but insist upon only taking part in
live programmes which would give her a chance to avoid such
contretemps. Yet, as her friends point out, Mary Whitehouse too
often lays herself open to a 'send up'. When in November 1974
she had her first column published in *TV Life* (a companion
paper to *TV Times*) the *Guardian* pointed out that the issue
featured on the front cover an item labelled 'Peter Ustinov on
sex and the fat man' and another by the actress Diana Rigg on
'Why not be a dirty old woman?'

In March 1970, she had also fallen for what appears—at
least in retrospect—to be another attempt to 'send her up'.
Granada TV invited her to visit Denmark with *World in Action*
to look at the permissive society there to see 'if this is what we
want for Britain'. She was promised a meeting with the Minister
of Justice who had sponsored the bill legalising pornography in

Denmark, the Chief of Police and others—some for, some against an openly permissive culture. She found it an agonising decision to make—but Malcolm Muggeridge, by now a friend and adviser and an experienced TV personality, strongly advised her to go. 'Destroy the Denmark myth, Mary,' he told her. She was promised that she would not be taken to the Sex Fair or filmed looking at pornography or indeed forced to engage in any conversation against her will, all of which promises were kept. Ray Gauer, a researcher for the US Presidential Commission on Obscenity and Pornography who had already visited Denmark, supplied her with certain relevant facts and information. Armed with this—and with her own strong beliefs—she took off for Copenhagen where she duly saw the Minister, a Lutheran woman pastor, and a pornographic publisher who claimed that his reasons for practising his profession were purely 'therapeutic'. Her confrontation with Dr Burl Kutschinsky, a criminologist who had carried out some research for the US Commission (but whose findings had been totally disregarded by them), proved a notable triumph. The doctor, who apparently held left-wing views, showed Mary and her camera team a chart allegedly proving that sex crimes in Copenhagen had decreased since the repeal of the national obscenity laws. If Mary Whitehouse had not been so well prepared, she would have lost her case right there but she managed to retrieve the situation brilliantly. She asked: (1) was the decrease not accounted for by the fact that the sale of pornography was no longer a crime? (2) was it not true that behaviour normally regarded as criminal was not now being reported to the police? (3) as pre-marital sex was now regarded as 'normal', was it not difficult for a girl who had already lost her virginity to claim statutory rape? To Mary's astonishment, when Kutschinsky had to agree to her points, the Granada team became very despondent. Asked why the gloom, she was told that the 'interviews have gone your way and it won't do'.

To Mary Whitehouse, this remark bore only the most sinister

of interpretations. In fact, it was no more than an example of her naivety. Like many people, she sometimes misunderstands the mechanics of television. Production teams have, in general, far more editorial control over their material than the majority of viewers imagine. Producers, directors and cameramen have their own ideas of what constitutes 'good television'; and people who have never been inside a studio would be baffled by their standards. Directors and cameramen are obsessed by the 'look' of the picture staring at the images they have framed on the small screen like aspiring Michelangelos. Secondary in importance seems to come the actual *material*. The classic test of 'good television' is whether the material is sensational, disturbing or merely soporific. What the Granada team were obviously hoping for in Denmark was a good confrontation, with Mary Whitehouse, hopefully, coming out the loser.

It was on the final day of this trip that Mary Whitehouse picked up an innocent-looking magazine in the bookstall of her hotel and suffered one of the greatest shocks of her life. When she opened the magazine it turned out to be full of hard core pornographic photographs which almost literally had her reeling. She admits that the images were so pervasive and corrupting that she found it hard to discard them from her mind and was so upset, according to Polly Bennett, that on her return home she had to 'ask the Lord to cleanse her'. She felt absolutely degraded and could picture the effect such photographs might have on the minds of adolescents.

Her ordeal, however, was still far from over. Feeling cheated of sensational stuff, the production crew now put a series of questions to her. By any reasonable standards, these questions seem pretty appalling. One crew man described some of the kinky practices he and his wife indulged in—would Mary Whitehouse disapprove of them? 'That's not for me to say,' she replied.

'What was wrong with pornography, anyway? Had she ever seen any? Would she describe it? What if your own husband turned to porn?' That a bunch of hard-bitten, cynical men should so bait a sensitive woman must appear incredible. That was not the end of the ordeal. The results of the film were upsetting to her. The film, she claims, depicted her as a mild little woman—sometimes looking almost deformed—who seemed lost and totally out of her depth. The film had been edited in such a way as to cut out most of her pointed questioning. She 'proves' her view by pointing out that Kutschinsky's chart alleging that there had been a decrease in sex crimes was given considerable prominence but that most of her penetrating questions were either fudged or left out completely. As a result many press critics naturally sympathetic to her claimed she had been 'too soft'. In fact, since Mary Whitehouse's visit, Denmark's 'experiment' in sexual freedom appears to have created more problems than it solved for the growth in the porn trade has drawn together criminal, pornographic and drug-trafficking elements and created a massive police problem.

Partly as a result of the film, however, Mary Whitehouse had become a national celebrity. On her return from Denmark William Hardcastle invited her to appear on his BBC radio show and from there she rushed off to Birmingham as the guest of Sir Lew Grade (who welcomed her with a kiss) for the formal opening of ATV's new studios by Princess Alexandra. The film on Copenhagen eventually went out to several countries, including Denmark and New Zealand.

There were fresh pressures from all quarters—particularly after her book on the Clean-Up Campaign was published. She was forced to listen to a stream of personal abuse from the playwright Vincent Tilsey during a discussion held at a comprehensive school; deal with the threat of a libel action by Dr Alex Comfort; stave off a group of businessmen who wanted to use VALA as a 'cover' to apply for an ITV contract (and who treated her to some considerable abuse when she refused on the grounds that she would never lend herself to any such project);

read that her mind was 'obscene' in the opinion of the *Freethinker*. When she arrived at a London hotel to address a meeting of young people police warned her that they had had a telephone call threatening to beat her up and wreck her meeting (a former high-ranking policeman had already warned her never to come to London on her own or accept invitations to lunch or dinner without first checking her host's credentials); and there was also the knowledge that a round-the-clock surveillance was being kept on the flats of two of her sons with the objective, seemingly, of catching them in compromising situations. There was a demand for money—accompanied by the threat that if she did not pay up, filthy stories would be circulated about her, her family and members of VALA. The *Financial Times* proclaimed that she was a 'little Canute'. Hostile reporters smuggled themselves into a VALA meeting in the guise of belonging to a religious organisation! It seemed that somewhere there was a department of dirty tricks which would, whether by physical or mental intimidation, browbeat her to the ground. For Mary Whitehouse, life in Britain was far from being the tolerant, sophisticated, civilized business that most Englishmen liked to think it was; light-years removed from those admirable concepts of English society that Anglophiles all over the world constantly praised. That dissent from current trends should arouse such calumny, hate and viciousness genuinely surprised her, and the physical and psychological damage was considerable. Her face aged ten years within three and the strain of it all began to tell. As she noted in her diary, 'This is the Cross—to realise there is no glamour, no appreciation to be asked or expected, nothing but ridicule, pain and loss. Friendship there is, and love, but even this does not touch the central core of loneliness in a battle of this kind.' It was a stony path she had chosen to tread and as she emphasises herself, it was only faith that kept her going. Whatever her opponents might think, believe or feel about Mary Whitehouse, she was unquestionably sincere and she had paid a fair price for her right to be heard. We know that during these periods of stress she had, besides her husband, only two things to sustain her: her belief in God and, on another level, the relief she obtained from the English countryside. In all her poems and prose, her overwhelming love for nature is dominant and makes it all the easier to understand why she demands that television should more often reflect the beautiful rather than the sordid. For some people, after all, the need for beauty is as compelling a force as the need felt by others to 'change the world'.

Yet despite these slings and arrows, despite the continuing refusal of the BBC authorities, its chairman, Lord Normanbrook and its Director-General, Sir Hugh Greene, to allow her organisation any standing or even to meet her or a deputation, important and respected figures in Britain were already prepared to have their names associated, however loosely, with hers. 'Bill' Deedes was a man of authority and not even the most radical could accuse him of being a crank; he had been the principal speaker at VALA's first annual convention in 1966, but who could follow him? When Mary Whitehouse awoke early one morning, she claims to have heard a name literally ringing in her head: Malcolm Muggeridge.

In May 1967, Muggeridge was regarded as one of England's wittiest and most acidulous minds, a man who knew all about the left wing because he had once been a member himself. Muggeridge's decision to address VALA's annual convention was a considerable triumph for Mary Whitehouse. BBC and ITV cameras were both there together with a formidable corps of newspaper reporters. Muggeridge declared with all the passion at his command, 'I am absolutely convinced that our civilisation will rush down the Gadarene slope which others have slipped down before, if we adhere to the notion that the image of life is not God but pigs in a trough. If life is pigs in a trough . . . then of course it does not matter much what you show on TV. If that were life, if *Till Death Us do Part* is life, I cannot see that there would be anything to do but to commit suicide.'

Mary Whitehouse had certainly proved that when it came to

manipulating the media, to understanding the springs and actions of propaganda, that she had learned the game. She had proved that anyone who is determined enough and sincere enough can get a hearing and that not even the BBC has the power to silence them. She had proved that if she were nothing more than a crank, then a considerable proportion of the British population were also cranks and that they did not exclude some of its most articulate and intellectual members.

CHAPTER EIGHT

Mary Meets Lord Hill

It seems almost incredible that Mary Whitehouse's first major appearance on TV was as recently as October, 1967. *Talkback* was a notable landmark in her career.

Her appearance arose out of an incautious remark by Stuart Hood, then one of the BBC's top executives, to the effect that the great majority of people who wrote in to the BBC were 'cranks' and even 'pathologically obscene'. It is, perhaps, typical of Mary Whitehouse's methods that she not only phoned the BBC to ask for an opportunity to refute Hood's remarks but also took the precaution of writing to Lord Hill, the new chairman, at the same time. Later Hugh Greene was to inform the critic Milton Shulman that he had been personally responsible for seeing that she was invited—until, then, of course, his attitude had been that her organisation represented nobody but themselves; but nevertheless the invitation cannot be seen as any breach of that principle. *Talkback* was the nearest attempt the BBC has yet made to allow ordinary viewers a public say about programmes. And as events transpired, few risks were taken.

Mrs Whitehouse says that she was led to believe that as VALA's representative she would be accorded a position of importance among the 'experts' flanking Stuart Hood. Instead, when she actually got into the studio, she found that she was merely one of a panel—and a hostile one at that. Nevertheless, despite appearing to hold a minority view about BBC programmes in general, she did manage to get a lot off her chest and even to slip in a call for an independent broadcasting council. Ten months earlier, her hopes of exerting a really

significant influence on British television had been raised when
Major James Dance, MP for Bromsgrove, Worcestershire (and
chairman of VALA from 1966 till his death in 1971) told her
that the Association appeared to have achieved a dramatic
breakthrough with the BBC: he had been invited by Lord
Normanbrook to lunch at Broadcasting House.

At that meeting a week later, Normanbrook—according to
Mary Whitehouse to whom James Dance had given the details
—mentioned that a 'total rift' existed between himself and Sir
Hugh Greene. He said that he was deeply concerned both about
the BBC and the country. His 'main purpose in proposing the
meeting' was his anxiety to do everything 'possible to bring
about an improvement in standards and re-establish public
confidence in the BBC'. Lord Normanbrook agreed that there
was a need for much closer co-operation between the BBC and
the public. And then—and this matter is still very much in the
realm of controversy—Normanbrook, having indicated that he
was interested in the idea of a proper Viewers' and Listeners'
Council, asked Dance whether Mary Whitehouse would be
prepared to set up such a Council. A condition was that any
such Council should consist of a representative cross-section of
British society and not just members of National VALA.
Another condition was that everything should be carried
through with the utmost secrecy.

Both Normanbrook and Dance are now dead and are unable
to confirm Mary Whitehouse's report of these events. She has no
doubt about the message delivered to her by Dance. She says
that she found Normanbrook's suggestion both flattering and
flabbergasting. She admits that it took her 'several weeks to get
adjusted to the idea that the chairman of the BBC should have
approached me in this way' (she still retains a certain naïve
reverence for these functionaries) and, indeed, would sometimes
shake Ernest awake in the middle of the night to ask him if her
good luck were really true. As she puts it with some humour,
Ernest would growl, 'Yes, of course it is—now go back to sleep!'

In the weeks and months that followed, she approached 'an impressive and representative group of men and women all eminent in their own sphere' and obtained the consent of many. Before she could complete the job, however, Lord Normanbrook died. On November 9, Lord Hill, the new chairman, received a deputation from National VALA consisting of Mary herself, James Dance (as chairman of VALA) and the Reverend David Mingard, at that time vice-chairman of the organisation. Lord Hill, according to his own memoirs, and Mary Whitehouse, according to her own account, found themselves at once at odds over what Normanbrook had actually said to James Dance. Hill insists that Normanbrook had 'resisted a suggestion that VALA should have a special position in an advisory capacity to the BBC on the grounds that it was an undemocratic body'. Mrs Whitehouse, according to Hill, said that certain changes had now been made, that it was a democratic body and that she took it from 'Lord Normanbrook's letter' that VALA would now be accorded special advisory status. 'I rejected the argument as I did the interpretation she put upon my predecessor's letter, making it plain that no organisation would have a special position in relation to the BBC. Her organisation was entitled to have its views considered as well as any others.'

There is some common ground between Mary Whitehouse and Lord Hill on the matter. They did meet on November 9. Hill did turn down the idea of any special role for VALA. But what is all this nonsense about a 'Normanbrook letter'? There never was any letter, she insists; the idea was never committed to writing. Indeed, she says, it was clear when her deputation met Lord Hill that not even so much as a memorandum of the conversation between Normanbrook and James Dance existed. Hill quickly made his position clear; whether the idea had ever been mooted or not, he was not prepared to implement it. There was nothing in the constitution of the BBC that allowed for such a Council—and anyway there already existed Advisory Councils to the BBC. He suggested that the best thing VALA could do was to forward their protests about material to him and he could take action where he considered it necessary.

When Mary Whitehouse made her version of the Norman-brook-Dance conversation public in 1971, the BBC departed from its usual practice sufficiently to release 'confidential notes' made by Normanbrook to the press. These claimed that immediately following his talk with Major Dance in December 1966 Lord Normanbrook had written down the minutes of the meeting in his own hand and headed it 'Note for Record'. In some respects, it proves a fascinating record of how it is possible for people to read into a conversation exactly what they want to read.

The Note, the BBC emphasised, contained no reference to any rift between Normanbrook and Greene. By itself, this would hardly constitute a rebuttal of Mary Whitehouse's version; the likelihood that Normanbrook would commit to writing any account of his feelings towards Greene or vice versa is hardly credible. The absence of any reference to a 'rift', therefore, neither proves nor disproves that it existed.

According to Normanbrook's note, the idea of the lunch was to have a confidential 'off the record' talk about the relations between the BBC and Mrs Whitehouse. According to Norman-brook, however, Major Dance recognised that the Clean-up campaign 'had got off on the wrong foot and had been too extreme and too sweeping in its denunciations of BBC programmes'. Dance might easily have put forward such a view— it is one with which Mary Whitehouse herself agrees wholeheartedly today. Dance then apparently suggested that VALA might be persuaded to 'adopt a more responsible attitude'. Normanbrook apparently concurred with this and explained that his main reason for declining to meet Mrs Whitehouse was that 'it was impossible for any responsible public corporation to enter into serious discussions with people who attacked its policy and performance in such extreme and irresponsible terms'. Normanbrook insisted that he 'had never found any evidence to suggest that she was speaking in any representative capacity. She seemed to be voicing no other opinion than her own'. He added that the BBC received many other letters which were considered and answered but that it did not regard itself as obliged to meet in person individuals who 'wish to express a purely personal point of view'. He then added that a different position 'might arise' if the Association was so constituted as to have some kind of representative capacity. 'If in addition to its new chairman (Major Dance) it also formed a council of responsible people and particularly if it built up some machinery for collecting representative views then it might be profitable for the BBC to hold some discussions with it on general questions on programme standards.' Normanbrook concluded that Major Dance agreed to explore these possibilities and said he thought there might be a council of about a dozen people nominated by representative organisations. He agreed that such a council would then be in a position to speak with much greater authority.

To an impartial observer this BBC account has a ring of truth about it and it is easy to see how a slightly different emphasis might be given to the remarks just out of enthusiasm. Mary Whitehouse appeared to be mistaken when she claimed that the release of Normanbrook's notes amounted to 'smear tactics' by some BBC chiefs to discredit her. 'I am prepared to stand by my statement on this private discussion between the two men,' she announced the day after the notes had been released. 'To suggest that this part of the conversation never took place is a smear on both of them and myself. The interesting thing is that these two men are dead. Someone at the BBC is not giving a true picture. They say they have their notes for the record. I have my notes for my record.'

Nonetheless, the weight of the evidence, however circumstantial, leans against Mrs Whitehouse. Sir Robert Lusty, Vice-chairman to Normanbrook, refuted her version in a letter to *The Times*. Lusty claimed that 'there was no such rift, nor any such secrecy'. The Board of Governors was 'always willing to consider representations from Mrs Whitehouse, provided she could explain who exactly it was she represented and that the constitution of her so-called council could be explained'. Lusty's view has to be given considerable weight—but one may question the BBC's refusal to meet Mary Whitehouse because she was unable 'to explain who exactly it was she represented'. It would seem that a sprawling Corporation such as the BBC needs to be reminded that the importance of any statement lies in its fundamental truth and not in the number of people who support it.

However, Mary Whitehouse, whose interpretation of the Normanbrook-Dance talk depends wholly on what Major Dance, possibly with the best of intentions, told her, comes out of the incident as the loser. Although she was disappointed she now feels that any Viewers and Listeners Council envisaged by Normanbrook would simply have become 'part and parcel of the BBC "establishment" '. She now claims that Lord Hill's attitude was, in the end, a relief.

But it failed to dampen her ardour in any way. In his book, *Behind the Screen*, Hill adopts a semi-paternalistic, semi-patronising attitude towards Mary Whitehouse as befits a *basso profundo* politician; if not an outright giggle, the lady is at least the source of some amusement. 'I had a little midsummer fun with that frequent and regular correspondent of mine, Mrs Whitehouse', he observed. Mrs Whitehouse is not above making herself mildly absurd at times—she is fully aware of the risks but feels that the likelihood of being made to look ridiculous is outweighed by the fact that evil-doers are at the same time made aware that she is always there, waiting to show them up. Bill Deedes admits that he thinks her 'judgment in what to attack and when to attack is frequently at fault. She very often takes on very small targets with very large guns and thereby loses firepower against the bigger target which emerges later'. She has even alienated some staunch members of the middle-classes by attacking a children's programme on the grounds that the attitudes displayed were latently homosexual! Nor did the public quite fall in behind her over the *Exit on Main Street* and the *Ding-a-ling* controversies.

She will never quite understand why seemingly sensible members of the public should have scoffed at her stand on these songs; she recognises that the pornographers are constantly pushing the threshold of public tolerance a little bit further, eroding standards almost imperceptibly so that they can claim 'What's so terribly wrong about this? After all, hasn't such-and-such already happened and, anyway, aren't people more adult these days?' Mary Whitehouse understands the technique only too well and it was with this in mind that she wrote to Lord Hill to protest against *Exit on Main Street*. By this time, Kenneth Tynan had managed to slip in his four-letter word on TV and the *Guardian* had embarked on the process of making it an OK word in print. 'Dear Lord Hill,' she wrote, 'I understand that the new Rolling Stones record, *Exit on Main Street*, is being played on Radio One. This record uses four-letter words. Although they are somewhat blurred, there's no question about what they are meant to be. Surely you will understand the concern felt about this matter for surely it is no function of the BBC to transmit language which, as was shown in a late court case, is still classed as obscene. The very fact that this programme is transmitted primarily for young people would, one would have thought, demanded more and not less care about what is transmitted. I would be grateful if you would look into this matter.'

Hill's reply was bucolicly jocose: 'Dear Mrs Whitehouse, thank you for your letter in which you allege that the tracks from the Rolling Stones *Exit on Main Street* played on Radio One uses four-letter words. I have this morning listened with great care to both tracks played on Radio One. I have listened to them at a fast rate, a medium rate and a slow rate and although my hearing is excellent I did not hear any offending four-letter words whatsoever. Could it be that believing the offending words to be there and zealous to discover them, you imagined what you did not hear? Yours sincerely, . . .'

Hill's was an attitude that still prevails in many broadcasting quarters. Yet as Mary Whitehouse points out, 'One has only to read the pop music magazines of the time to discover that four-letter words were, indeed, used. And at the time of the brouhaha over Ding-a-ling, *Melody Maker* carried an article listing which obscene records had been banned and which had been allowed through. And they listed Ding-a-ling as an obscene one that had got through.'

Hill's appointment as chairman of the BBC has been seen as Harold Wilson's move to cut Hugh Greene down to size. Under Lord Reith, the powers of the Chairman and Board of Governors of the BBC and the Director-General had become clearly defined. Neither the Chairman nor the Board were expected to do anything but lay down the broad lines of BBC policy. In the hands of the Director-General resided all operational power. He and he alone was responsible for the manner in which those broad lines were implemented. Chairman and Board members did not interfere; the D-G became, in effect, the all-highest. With the appointment of Baron Hill of Luton (widely known as 'Charlie, the radio doctor'), it became evident that the Labour party, increasingly disenchanted with a BBC regime which believed itself independent of party or politics, had decided to end the Reithian system. The BBC almost got as its boss Herbert Bowden, who had been Labour's chief whip. In the end, however, it suited Wilson's book much better that the job of cutting down Greene should be carried out by a former Tory politician rather than a Labour one.

With Hill's appointment in July 1967, Mary Whitehouse and her Association really went to town in their attempt to secure Sir Hugh Greene's resignation. Mary had long been sure that until Greene walked through the portals of Broadcasting House for the last time, the BBC would continue to undermine the British nation. So the next issue of *The Viewer and Listener*, VALA's newsletter, carried an open letter once again calling on Greene to resign. As before, the call had no obvious or immediate effect.

Rather more significant, however, was a letter which Mary wrote just before Christmas, 1967, protesting that certain lines in the Beatles' *Magical Mystery Tour*, a short film intended to be among the BBC's major Christmas 'attractions', were indecent. Apart from an acknowledgement of her letter, her protest was seemingly ignored and the song went on the air still containing the offending lines. It was not until Kenneth Adam, a former Director of BBC TV, published his memoirs a few years later that it transpired that her protest had created the first serious breach between Hill and Greene—the beginning, in fact, of a series of battles over who exactly *should* control the BBC, Chairman or Director-General, which ended with Greene's resignation. According to Adam, Hill was insistent that the indecent lines should be dropped or the whole film cancelled. Greene refused to do either and when Hill demanded to know what would happen if he gave a specific instruction, Greene replied that he would be unable to accept it. A clash between the two men, of course, was inevitable, for it was Hill's resolve—and presumably the Government's—that the power of the Director-General should be curbed.

Mrs Whitehouse, of course, does not claim that she was, to any appreciable degree, responsible for the departure of Hugh Greene. There were many other forces out to get Sir Hugh Greene's head—from the *Sunday Express* which accused him of harbouring Communists or near-Communists on his staff, to the political front benches of both major British parties which felt that the BBC was far too independent. On July 16, 1968, Sir Hugh Greene's resignation was finally announced. It can scarcely be doubted that Mary Whitehouse felt that the Lord had smiled on her.

It was a prodigious schedule for a middle-aged woman, apart from the drain of energy caused by a whole series of psychological assaults from all quarters, ranging from personal abuse (the inimitable Sir Gerald Nabarro calling her 'a hypocritical old bitch' on a television programme) to attacks on everything she held dear and delivered in various guises. Her 'season', which still coincides with the TV 'season' (between September and June when TV attracts its largest audiences and TV programmers put on their newest wares), increasingly took her away from home and she spent most of her time travelling round Britain addressing 'meetings of every kind'. One day she might address a meeting at the House of Lords; the next one at Brighton. Thence to Aberdeen to be interviewed for Grampian TV; to Dundee for a speech to the Ladies Dinner Club; topped off by a thirty-mile drive to Crieff to speak at 'a coffee morning'. Five years after she had launched her campaign, her schedule was much fuller than any film star's and possibly as well filled as that of the Prime Minister. She often had to be absent from home for several days on end, often addressing as many as three meetings in a single day. Once, after standing for a half-hour to address her audience and then standing for another half-hour to answer their questions, her leg began to swell and she was in such pain that she was forced to place all her weight on the other leg and stand like a stork; mercifully the meeting was cut short by the chairman, a doctor, and she was rushed to hospital for an X-ray.

Even a brief perusal of her diary shows how alert Mary Whitehouse is to the importance of projecting a good personal image (some allowance must also be made for the natural feminine desire to look as well as she can). 'Good report in the local paper, but dreadful photo—oh dear!' she comments. Before appearing at Dundee Academy to take part in a debate before 300 Fifth and Sixth formers, she took care to remove the bandage round her swollen leg. 'If I hobbled in with that I'd have lost the debate before it even began!'

It was—and still is—a punishing task she had set herself. Travel by train, car, taxi. Speeches, debates, TV and radio appearances, constant interviews with press. Facing up to groups of hostile students at such places as Brighton Training College; being howled and jeered at Dundee station by a crowd of drunks. In between delivering speeches, she spent days in hotel bedrooms typing out 'extracts from last night's address at the Parish Church and sending them off to religious weeklies before going on to tea party for about forty clerics and their wives.'

There are also the private worries and thoughts: 'Insisted that we must not let ourselves be termed "reactionaries". Far from it—we were visionaries—we too "had a dream", the 1970s were meant to be "an era of informed, responsible public opinion in which everyone, whatever their background, could become involved".'

Psychologically, the strain was telling. There was her reaction to the BBC's decision to repeat an *Omnibus* programme about the pop scene called *All My Loving*, for example. This was an extraordinary show in which a pop singer simulated the sexual act with his guitar while part of the audience—according to the commentator—masturbated and shots of the singer were mixed in with scenes of sadistic brutality involving concentration camps, a Buddhist monk immolating himself, savage action from Vietnam and so on. She consulted VALA's solicitors on the feasibility of bringing a private prosecution against both the producer and the BBC. Despite a solicitor's warning letter, the BBC repeated the programme. The night of the repeat she went to bed, according to her diary, 'Feeling heavily burdened by the *All My Loving* affair. How could we, realistically, finance a private action against the BBC, and what is a woman of my age doing getting involved in masculine obscenity like this, anyway?'

Asked on one occasion how she reacted to the 'truly awful things people said about her', she replied, 'You couldn't do this

kind of work if you minded what people said about you. One of
the silly suggestions that has been made is that anybody who was
concerned with the present obsession with sex in our society
must have had an unsatisfactory sex life. Well, I see it as exactly
the opposite; it is *because* my sex life has been so satisfactory that
I have no problems. I feel free.'

There are, of course, chinks in her armour. Sometimes she is
more easily wounded by slighting references to her physical
appearance than by onslaughts on her opinions. What hurt her
almost as much as anything else about the film of her trip to
Denmark was that some of the shorts made her look 'almost
deformed'. Much later, when she attended the Little Red
School Book trial, she bought a new hat—'a really choice little
hat, actually'—only to pick up a paper and see it referred to as
her *familiar* hat. 'I thought: *Blow me!*' she declared. So she is not
without her small vanities—if that is any consolation to her
opponents.

Mary Whitehouse admits that she started out simply to 'clean-
up' TV—spurred by the irreverence of the late-night 'satire'
shows, and by the kind of plays put out by the BBC. It is,
perhaps, a sign of the times that although her objections were
against the *violence* of certain programmes as much as anything
else, her opponents—and, indeed, members of the general
public who did not bother to analyse the matter too closely—
immediately interpreted the cry of 'censorship' which rose up to
mean that she wanted to censor sex. In a sense, of course, everything depends upon what is meant by censorship and sex. Was
it an act of censorship *not* to show full frontal nudity or the
sexual act in detail? Or was it simply a matter of recognising
that there are many areas of human behaviour—the performance of the natural functions, particularly—which are areas we
all prefer to blanket from our thoughts? Was it not possible that
the sexual act had as many claims to be practised in privacy as
the act of excreting? And did Mary Whitehouse's opponents

really seriously mean it when they claimed that she wanted *sex* banned on TV?

So far as I can discover, Mary Whitehouse does not object to any programme that suggests men are different from women, that there is attraction between them; that kisses and other tender caresses are not a preliminary to the act of copulation. She argues that she is against making the sexual act public, debasing something that, at its best, can be an intense and unique expression of human love and tenderness. She stands by those who prefer to equate sex with love, and against those who seem to treat it as an animal function no more significant than eating or drinking—a regression, she would maintain, to the behaviour of primitive man. In short, Mrs Whitehouse is not in favour of a return to the ethics of the Stone Age.

However there were among those who controlled departments of the media some, for possibly good reasons, who wished the latter attitude to spread. As she says herself, 'it didn't take long to discover that the media are indivisible, and that what happens on the stage, and in films, is inevitably reflected on television'. By labelling a programme, 'documentary' or 'serious discussion' or 'art' or 'reality', offerings of the commercial cinema and stage, made by entrepreneurs searching desperately for any sensational device that would entice paying audiences from their TV sets, began to be shown on TV in extract; thus people were regaled in their parlours with extracts from *Hair* and *Oh Calcutta!* whether or not they felt inclined to visit those shows. Even the late Kenneth Allsop, an old-fashioned reporter, was unable to resist the trend towards permissiveness and made some programmes in Denmark including one which showed the making of a 'blue' film in rather explicit detail. In September 1970, the BBC, in a programme ostensibly about marriage, showed full frontal male nudity for the first time. At once Mrs Whitehouse swung into action but the BBC replied: 'You ask on whose recommendation the decision to show full frontal nudity was taken. There is, in fact, very rarely a precise moment at which decisions about *matters of taste* (my italics) of this kind are taken. It becomes clear, as time passes, that standards change and that what was thought to be unacceptable yesterday is more tolerantly regarded today. The sense of violation which can be aroused in one year is quite dormant in the next. These changes do not take place at the same place in all areas of programmes, however, and we believe the important tests to be those of the context and motive. For that reason, we consider the documentary setting of the present incident to be relevant. There is little doubt that nudity in a variety show would attract large audiences but it would, of course, outrage a great many people and its inclusion could not, therefore, be contemplated. In the case of other kinds of programmes, however, the issue is by no means as clear cut. Our experience is that audiences in general do not have a very violent reaction to the display of the naked human body, provided that it is displayed in a way that is seemly.' The letter was interpreted by Mrs Whitehouse as a complete giveaway; someone in the BBC felt that what was 'unacceptable yesterday' was 'more tolerantly regarded today'. This was exactly the point she had been for long trying to make: that 'standards' were constantly being eroded or slowly chipped away, the viewer steadily softened up. It was a technique which she understood—and if the public were too apathetic or too undiscerning to heed it, that was hardly her fault.

Mary Whitehouse would argue, in general, that people are not sufficiently alert. Now and then she would provide evidence to reinforce this opinion. It did not need a great deal of discerning intelligence to realise that the apostles of pornography fell into neat groupings. There were, firstly, those who saw a profit in the business—the publishers of 'dirty' books, producers of 'blue' movies and so on; secondly, there were those, homosexuals or lesbians or simple libertines, often placed in positions of authority within the media, who hoped for a 'more tolerant' climate of opinion for their own status; and thirdly, there were those who saw in pornography—as they saw in the use of drugs

—a way of destroying the moral fibre of the younger western generation, thus undermining its will to resist political change or, if it came to a showdown, to fight for their country.

It was not very difficult to discern the kind of thinking behind many BBC TV plays, for example. Mrs Whitehouse was fortunate enough to find a letter in the *Sunday Times* which referred to a passage in *Cinema Documents*, a publication bearing the imprimatur of the Italian Communist party, which dealt with the party's attitude towards plays about sex. 'We are interested in encouraging this type of play' ran the document, 'and we are likewise prepared to praise actors of such plays as champions of artistic freedom. We want to encourage this sort of artistic production, and must lead people on to produce others that are, sexually speaking, more daring still, and that contain scenes that are downright scandalous. As a tactical policy, our aim is to defend an enterprise that is pornographic and entirely free from the restrictions of ordinary moral rules. They (directors and actors) are in effect like ants working voluntarily and without pay for us as they eat away at the very roots of their bourgeois society. Why should we stop them from their work? Why should we place obstacles in their path?'

CHAPTER NINE

Travelling the World

As National VALA became more and more of a British institution, Mary Whitehouse had her moments of triumph, of despair, of humiliation, of insult, of delight, She ploughed through the lot like a tank, always displaying a remarkable courage and stamina, and continually sustained by her belief that she was performing God's work.

There were the triumphs. Shortly after Sir Hugh Greene's resignation, for example, Lord Hill set up an independent Programme Complaints Commission and the ITA set up a new Complaints Review Board. There can be little doubt that Mary Whitehouse's activities had contributed to those decisions. The Pope received her at Castel Gandolfo and, after inquiring into such British concerns as the progress of the Festival of Light, bestowed his customary (if automatic) blessing upon her and her work. Another success was when no less a figure than David Frost consented to be guest speaker at VALA's 1969 annual convention.

It was, however, anything but a path of primroses all the time. During what was intended to be a quiet debate at an Essex school, a member of the BBC's religious department astonished her by describing her as 'a most dangerous woman'.

Nothing daunted she marched boldly into one university after another—Durham Union, Leicester, Cambridge, Aberystwyth. At Strathclyde, the students greeted her with a continual chant of 'Out, out, out!' At Aston she had to climb over the outstretched legs of milling students armed with posters, rattles and tin cans just to get to the platform. At Oxford, she had to listen to a tirade from a BBC producer who called her 'a fascist' and 'a reactionary'. At Birmingham, they kept on and on about *her* sex life. At Leicester Edward Bond, author of *Saved* (the play in which a baby is stoned to death) opened the proceedings by referring to the obscene graffiti written about her on the walls of gentlemen's lavatories; Bond also suggested that she was responsible for the Moors murders! For over forty minutes she tried to make her voice heard while the students turned the proceedings into a bear garden. 'It was like living in a madhouse,' she explained afterwards. 'Unreason took over and obscenities flew hard and fast the whole of the night. Students were crawling past me on their hands and knees. It was quite clear that they wanted to make me go away and all my natural self wanted to run a mile.

'But I knew I had to stay because I had to be a catalyst. I knew that if I stayed, some of the students would see which side they were on and whether they were for or against. An experience becomes *creative*, if you like, if you really do suffer in it. If I went there and didn't care two hoots, it would not have done a thing to anybody. Not really. So you don't have to be afraid to go where the dirt is.' Nonetheless, the debate had to be abandoned after forty minutes of ineffectual attempts to restore order.

Her experiences taught her a lot about the tactics used by the revolutionary Left. Now she prays that one day she will be able to 'explode with an amusing turn of phrase, the poverty of the (New Left's) case and the weakness of its strategy'.

At Bristol, in fact, she *was* able to turn a phrase against an *avant-garde* publisher. In a debate with John Calder who had attempted to publish a book about homosexuality called *Last Exit to Brooklyn*, she labelled Calder, a campaigner for the abolition of the present laws on obscenity, as a man who 'saw a censor under every bed'. Calder had like many of her opponents helped rather than hindered Mary Whitehouse's case. He declared that art did not make people 'better or worse'—which may or may not be true—and then tried to insist that 'books do not affect behaviour'; which, as Mary Whitehouse coolly pointed out, leave the Bible and *Das Kapital* looking rather anaemic.

It wasn't long before Mary Whitehouse found herself involved in controversy over the type of sex education proposed to be taught in British schools. On April 16, 1971, she accepted an invitation from Dr Martin Cole, a plant geneticist, to see his film *Growing Up* which had been made to give modern sex education to children in schools. Mary Whitehouse emerged from the preview cinema white-faced and angry, and she bluntly told reporters that it was 'a rotten film . . . which makes children no more than animals—"if you want sex, have it."'

She at once wrote to Dr Michael Ramsey, the Archbishop of Canterbury, asking him to give Christian guidance to the country and he issued a statement saying that since, 'the commentator in the film observes that sexual relations is sometimes a good practice for the development of young unmarried men and women . . . the film diverges from the Christian ideals of education and makes it unsuitable for use in schools.' The Archbishop added, 'While pornography is a great evil, a more insidiously dangerous evil is the infiltration of false values through the trivialisation of nudity and sex and the treatment of them for merely sensuous gratification.'

Cole, a controversial figure by anybody's standards, became the spokesman for the progressive viewpoint in at least two other radio programmes which dealt with sex education for the young. With more than a touch of exasperation, Mary Whitehouse demanded to know why Dr Martin Cole was 'considered the most suitable person to guide children'. He was neither a teacher, a doctor (of medicine) nor a psychiatrist so what were his qualifications? But Mary Whitehouse's opponents were able to make at least two good valid points against her. Ought not the views of articulate, intelligent men such as Martin Cole at least be heard? If he were wrong, then what harm was there in letting his errors be exposed? Secondly was Mary Whitehouse seriously suggesting that the BBC was a monolithic institution run by a Presidential figure at the top passing or rejecting every item that was to be broadcast? Mrs Whitehouse ignored the fact that programmes are often put together by teams of two or three people. Today, Mary Whitehouse recognises that many of the 'errors' committed by the BBC *are* the result of fallible or hasty actions made often by low-level operatives and are not necessarily a 'plot' by those responsible for the overall output of the Corporation.

It was inconceivable, of course, that she would stay out of the notorious Little Red School Book case which took place in 1971, having heard beforehand from contacts in Denmark that it contained material of a Maoist revolutionary nature and was full of obscenities. She at once drew the attention of the Director of Public Prosecutions to the publication but found that Scotland Yard, quite independently, had forestalled her. However, she sat for three days in the Lambeth court during the trial and when the magistrate declared the publisher guilty of 'possessing obscene material for gain', she came in for a barrage of hisses and abuse.

Again in 1971, she followed the prosecution of OZ, the underground paper, with close attention. The original sentences for Richard Neville, OZ's editor, was 15 months; James Anderson and Felix Dennis 12 and 9 months respectively. At the appeal Lord Widgery, the Lord Chief Justice, reduced their sentences to 6 months, suspended for 2 years, and cancelled a deportation order against Neville. The country-wide petition calling on the Government to revise the Obscenity Laws, which she together with VALA and Festival of Light supporters then drew up, is described in greater detail in chapter 13.

Her involvement in every aspect of pornography and permissiveness grew. When Ken Russell's controversial film *Dance of the Seven Veils* on Richard Strauss was screened, Fleet Street were on to her immediately afterwards ('I felt soiled watching the stuff' she told them), while *The World At One* radio show interviewed her and Russell on a question and answer basis. The *Sunday Express* and *Daily Telegraph* followed up her reactions and even the Americans got into the act with an interview on the subject of sex and violence on British TV.

Mary Whitehouse had set out to become a small if painful thorn in the side of the BBC—but by now she was threatening to ram a great big spike into their corporate body. She considered the possibility of taking legal action against the BBC on this count or that; but according to the Minister in charge of Communication the BBC were immune from prosecution because they were a corporation. She declared her intention of suing the Post Office who actually transmitted TV programmes, and made headlines throughout Fleet Street. When the BBC attempted to enter certain sex education films at the Catholic Film Festival at Monte Carlo, she sent a telegram to the Festival president pointing out that the films were banned from Catholic schools in Britain and that if they were to admit them to the Festival this would enable the BBC to renew their pressure on the Catholic authorities in Britain. Her name had by now become a household one.

In the last ten years, of course, her life has changed out of all recognition. She is no longer an obscure middle-aged provincial schoolmistress but a figure of some influence in this country, though whether for the good or not depends largely upon your viewpoint. In 1973 she toured Australia, one of the big events of her life. 'You know,' she says, 'I became better known in Australia in three and a half weeks than I did in Britain in ten years.'

Her Australian trip almost had to be cancelled. Earlier that year she and Ernest had spent their holidays in Gambia. Her friend Polly Bennett recalls that on her return Mary went down to Essex to address the annual meeting of the local branch of VALA (there are now some 28 branches throughout the country).

'She told me that she'd have to get to bed—she felt so ill. "My brain won't do anything." she said. Our local doctor, who's chairman of our branch, went up to see her and wrote out a prescription. But she wasn't well enough even to come down to dinner. She couldn't eat anything—and just lay there in the dark with her hands over her eyes. So I called an immediate prayer meeting—and believe it or not, she actually spoke at the meeting that same night. That's the kind of courage she has.'

Mary, in fact, had contracted malaria. By September 1973, when she was due to depart for Australia, she had more or less recovered, but still felt anaemic as a result of her illness. But the arrangements for her tour were so far advanced that she found it difficult to cancel them. Then at the last moment, Ernest became ill with blood pressure and when she realised that she would have to face the ordeal of the tour on her own she broke down in despair.

After a twenty-eight hour flight, she took on an immediate press and TV conference at her first stop in Darwin. She arrived, to complicate matters, when there was a postal strike, an electricity strike and an airport strike. She managed to get to Brisbane, but found there was no way she could get to Sydney by scheduled flight. So she hired a small Cessna light aircraft, and the trip turned out to be the wildest experience of her life. The plane had no radar; so the pilot asked her to keep her eyes peeled to prevent the Cessna running into other aircraft. Then Sydney airport refused them permission to land so they had to come down in the outback and re-fuel at a single-pump airstrip; but the pump would not work because of the electricity strike! In the end, they re-fuelled and Sydney relented, provided that they followed the coast all the way and never flew above 500 feet. At one point, they had to fly round a lighthouse! Meanwhile on the ground, all Australia listened in as breathless radio commentators kept track of her progress, reporting her flight as though it were an episode from *The Perils of Pauline*.

She certainly never had a dull moment. To get to Adelaide she had to sit on the inky floor of an aeroplane used to transport newspapers. At the University the police were called out to deal with the rioting students. One day she gave no fewer than *ten* radio and TV interviews. On another day she foiled an attempt by a pornographic publisher to subpoena her to appear in his trial; the defendant wanted her to give evidence that his publication was mild compared with those permitted in Britain!

Back in England there were new problems to tackle. When a blue-film maker was acquitted by an all-male jury, Mary Whitehouse, backed by National VALA, stepped in with a demand that should appeal to every woman's liberationist. She demanded that the Attorney-General should amend the law to ensure that half of all juries should consist of women. She declared to the press that the police had told her that it was the 'general strategy' in obscenity cases nowadays for the defence to object to prospective women jurors. 'Women are far more sensitive in this field than men,' she emphasised. 'I see no reason why any jury should not be fifty per cent women. Anything else is certainly out of sympathy with the sex equality law which is just coming in. Women are used in pornography and women often suffer greatly at the hands of men who are addicted to it, and they should be able to play their part in controlling it through the process of law. If the defendant objects to a particular woman juror, she should be replaced by another woman, and not by a man.'

It is this kind of reasonable and logical argument that tends to infuriate her opponents. Had Germaine Greer or some such woman called for fifty per cent of women on *all* juries, the idea would have been greeted with enthusiasm. When Mary Whitehouse put forward this plea on behalf of women she was suspected of trying to extend the right to exercise censorship.

The 'progressive' minded who have had the tide with them for more than a decade now find it increasingly difficult to steamroller their views through without Mary Whitehouse barring their way, however difficult it is to 'prove' that obscenity and pornography harm society as a whole.

It is precisely because she realises how difficult it is to put across her argument effectively that Mrs Whitehouse is prepared, like her opponents, to use any weapon that comes to hand. She thought long and hard before agreeing to contribute a column to a publication run by the ITV companies but finally decided that in this modern age 'one had to use whatever weapons came to hand'. Thus she began yet another career—this time doing what one newspaper described as writing 'an agony column'. It is perhaps typical of Mrs Whitehouse's keen antennae—which can now detect the slightest nuance—that she felt that this was a less than objective description; that once again those in Fleet Street who stood on the opposite side of the fence and who wished her ill, had tried to deliver yet another dig.

CHAPTER TEN

Mary's Achievements

One of the chief difficulties in dealing with the phenomenon of Mary Whitehouse with any degree of objectivity is that she has plunged head first into an area of debate where no truly objective opinions or statistics are obtainable.

One critic, Keith Brace, has written, 'Many commentators, including myself, who were originally completely opposed to her campaign, would now agree that she was justified in asking what the effects of television were on the audience and condemning at least some of the programmes and trends she did condemn. Some of the changes she called for have certainly taken place; the resignation of Hugh Greene; and the reluctant agreement of the BBC to form a grievances committee, which she regards merely as a gesture, although in the right direction. What is most obviously lacking . . . is any real sense of historical and social background. Mrs Whitehouse deplores materialism; but she never questions our social, economic and political structure with its emphasis on material rewards, never suggests social or political reforms that might improve our moral life. She never asks herself if today's excessive sexual freedom among the young may be an inevitable revolt against the excessive sexual restrictiveness of her generation (and mine).'

In the end, of course, one begins to despair; every commentator tends to dodge the central issues and gets lost in his own prejudices. Mary Whitehouse and her generation, surely, were all agog about sex in the nineteen-twenties and nineteen-thirties. Now exactly where was Keith Brace, in those days: in a monastery? Victoria and Albert were long since dead; hundreds of thousands of soldiers had sampled the delights of Gay Paree. Theirs was the generation of the Bright Young Things and their philosophy of 'Blazing Youth'. The Russians had had their revolution and most literate persons had dipped into Marx. Mary Whitehouse rightly condemns the myths largely invented by her opponents. The idea that the generation that came to puberty in the twenties and thirties was suffering from 'excessive sexual restrictiveness' may be believed by the post-Second World War Generation but it is rubbish to those of us who actually lived then.

Nor is it clear to me why Mrs Whitehouse really ought to be running around suggesting 'social or political reforms that might improve moral life'; or that she should question 'our social, economic and political structure'. Political reforms are an on-going matter at the best of times and if the introduction of the Welfare State and the National Health Service are not considered significant 'reforms', then the word has lost its meaning; anyway, is the implication here that Mary Whitehouse ought to enter Parliament? The fact is that while affluence and the general advance of technology has turned England into a nation of semi-detached house and two-car garage owners, the elementary rights of the individual have been consistently eroded. Bus conductors are now being murdered in London. Thugs rob or beat up old ladies, old men, women and girls on the London Underground. The thin veneer of civilisation that has kept the brute within all of us at bay has been deliberately cracked and we are back in the eighteenth century.

Mary Whitehouse and everything she stands for are vulnerable as she herself has declared. She and her association are prepared to 'make fools of themselves for the Lord' and she adds: 'that's basic. We felt we had to raise a flag and you don't know until you raise your flag, whether other people feel the same way as you do.'

Yet there is a curious inadequacy about those who shoulder the burden; almost as though English society was hopelessly split between those with a capacity to *think* and those quite incapable of it. Jilly Cooper, for instance, who writes a column for the *Sunday Times*, claims to have detected in Mary Whitehouse's campaign the beginning of a new Victorian age. 'Table legs will soon be covered up, and the fornication detector van will be policing the streets flushing out people without a sexual licence.' She finds Mrs Whitehouse's ideas 'sinister and chilling'; accuses her of an almost 'pathological disgust of pornography'—adding 'whatever that may be'. (If Jilly Cooper does not know what pornography is, how does she know whether Mrs Whitehouse's 'pathological disgust' is justified or not?) Mrs Cooper continues: 'One of the good things about the Sixties was that a great many people stopped feeling guilty about sex and started realising that feelings and desires they'd always been ashamed of were perfectly normal and common to other people. My main complaint about Mrs Whitehouse is she seems likely to re-create these feelings of guilt.' This is the kind of thinking that has Mary Whitehouse reaching for her Bible and offering up a prayer to the only Person who, presumably, can do anything about the mental processes that produce it. How many people stopped feeling guilty about sex in the sixties, for instance—that is, besides Jilly Cooper? How did this figure compare with the number of people who stopped feeling guilty about sex in the fifties or the forties or the thirties or the twenties, or in the seventeenth century? How about the guilty sex feelings at Nero's court? What has Mary Whitehouse's demand for a civilised level of public decency, an end to the exploitation and corruption of children and access to the media for those who believe in a morality based on traditional Christianity (the only one we have got), got to do with re-creating 'these feelings of (sex) guilt'?

Wilfred Greatorex is a TV writer-producer who has never felt the lash of Mary Whitehouse's attack because his work is well-crafted fiction and rarely strays into dangerous political, philosophical or moral waters. He represents a large body of middle-of-the-road writers and producers whose output forms a con-

siderable proportion of both BBC and ITV programmes. He sees
Mary Whitehouse as representing a narrow, puritanical tradition in English society. He considers her stance arrogant because
she can claim no statistical right to speak for millions in any
elected sense. Her work, he feels, tends to produce a curb on the
freedom of writers. He sees her activities as lessening 'the vitality'
of TV; of 'softening' it so that it becomes a bland, inhibited
medium 'softening its message to *her* morality, which is not the
morality of a lot of people today'. To his mind, she doesn't want
'people to have full information—and this at a time when society
is in a tremendously fluid state, the most fluid in my lifetime.'
To Greatorex's way of thinking—and it is a not uncommon view
among those who work in television—the real danger from Mary
Whitehouse arises from her desire to 'censor out' exciting and
exhilarating ideas and reduce television in Britain to the 'level of
pure pap'. Unlike Johnny Speight, who professes to believe that
Mary Whitehouse has had no discernible influence on British
television, Wilf Greatorex finds that 'there are a lot of people in
TV who are frightened for their jobs because of Mary Whitehouse. I've no doubt that the sheer noise which has come from
her has caused some writers to be inhibited, has made them go
easy. And the result? In come the trivia boys!'

Inside BBC Television Centre, the producer of a controversial
TV show turns the argument round the other way. 'I would
agree with Mr and Mrs Whitehouse in that I too share deep,
deep apprehensions that an outdated code of so-called democracy—what a laugh!—called Marxism, may take over this
country. I *will not* accept Marxism in this country! What we've
got to have is a philosophy for today—it may not be of the Left
and it may not be of the Right, it may reflect the present
Establishment view (and I number Hugh Scanlon and Jack
Jones as among the establishment figures today) or it may not—
but unless we reflect that philosophy in some way, unless we
hold up the mirror, there may be civil war in this country—or at
least civil disturbance. As to a BBC attitude—the BBC probably

employs some 600 producers all told. Some are of the Left, some of the Right and some are of the Centre and some hold their own individual views. As it is today, there is no single BBC attitude—and that is part of the Corporation's merit. What I am more concerned about is to see that no minority group is allowed to dictate to the BBC in a totalitarian manner because, as I see it, that will open the way to control by the politicians.'

It is now argued—and with some justification—that Mary Whitehouse *has* begun to set herself up as a Great Universal Nanny because her movement, which originally set out on a straightforward crusade against programmes she deplored on TV and radio has now so widened its interests as to take in almost every form of communication; but as she has explained, this was an inevitable consequence of the discovery that the media are indivisible. She argues, for example, that what is shown on today's West End screen, will be shown on national TV in five years time; which is why she fought Mrs Wistrich's unsuccessful move to abolish film censorship in London. No sooner had Mrs Wistrich failed, however, than Mary Whitehouse began pressing for a new Films Act on the grounds that censorship of films is *not nearly strict enough.*

The Secretary of the British Board of Film Censors, 1971–75, was Stephen Murphy, a middle-aged Scot who was criticised about the Board's decisions to pass such films as *The Clockwork Orange* and *Straw Dogs.* Murphy probably represented the type of individual whom Mary and her Association are most wary of, the kind of man whose lifestyle and experience set him apart, insulated him against the realities of life as it is really lived in Britain and from the standards of behaviour adhered to by most of its inhabitants. Mary and her colleagues, on the whole, are still suspicious of the kind of amoral, pseudo-sophisticated life led, they believe, by most of those working in the London media.

Murphy, indeed, tried to reach conclusions about whether a film is fit to be shown to the general public or not without basing his opinions on any moral code; a formidable task. He declares:

'I don't think there's anybody good enough or wise enough in British society today to know which morality is relevant to the way our children should lead their lives.' Are parents not going to bother to instruct their children? As he sees it, there are 'choices open to people'. He argues that his job was narrowed down to two things: (1) To ensure that the true artist working in a free society had the right to challenge preconceived ideas, and (2) that the public has a right to be protected—not against the artist with a burning desire to say things—but against those with no true artistic instinct who merely wish to copy an artist's idea in order to make money. He defends the Board's decision to pass *Clockwork Orange* (where one salacious scene is played out to a Rossini overture), by pointing out that the Board subsequently refused to pass no fewer than *four* imitations of *Clockwork Orange*—which seems to mean that his moral code is based on something called 'artistic integrity'. As a novelist I admire artistic integrity above most things, yet I confess I can find very little logic in an argument which accepts 'artistic integrity' as the basis of a morality and yet discounts the injunctions of the Ten Commandments (and what ever else stems from them).

Murphy's thinking had little or no connection with the Ten Commandments, except coincidentally. He felt that he was there simply to reflect 'intelligent public opinion. We are not here to lay down a morality universally true for everyone because those days are over—there is not a universally accepted public morality any more'. Murphy makes the point, of course, that one of the worst aspects of the twentieth century has been an attempt 'to suppress the thinking of literate, intelligent people'. On more technical grounds he argues that the advent of TV has forced every other medium of communication to face a new situation. Once, he says, it was the function of the cinema to provide escapist, middle-of-the-road entertainment—lightly tossing such masterpieces as *The Blue Angel* and *Un Carnet de Bal* among others into the wastepaper basket—but now the cinema industry has to adjust to a powerful new competitor. He seemed to think that the cinema was forced to provide material that is sufficiently exciting or spectacular to attract people away from their TV sets; and here one recognises the herculean task he has had to face. To have achieved this the cinema could easily have pushed the limits of sex exploitation even further than television does; and indeed, the cinema has recently tried to inject both *more* explicitly sexual scenes and *more* violence into its products. To balance the needs of an industry fighting to survive with the need to protect the minds of a small but inevitable percentage of the public who are irrationally swayed by what they see is perilous tight-rope walking. Murphy also believed that TV has been responsible for 'hurting people in the middle classes— people who have maintained a Hellenic–Hebraic society since the Renaissance' and who now have to face a world where a lot of people 'not brought up in the Hellenic–Hebraic civilisation tradition' and who are not all that well intellectually equipped, are told that there is a culture 'beyond that'. This culture is being projected particularly through television. What Mary Whitehouse and her Association is facing is 'an explosion into the middle class of concepts of society which have never been explored before'. Stephen Murphy personally found Mary Whitehouse 'enormously valuable'. He saw her as very good at putting the 'right-hand cultural viewpoint' (as opposed to the left-hand) and therefore helping him to 'shape the balance'. He did not believe that either the cinema or TV should be free to put 'every idea that the extremists want to put', for modern society needed 'certain inhibitions'. Mary Whitehouse represents those 'inhibitions' at one extreme, balancing those who wanted 'no inhibitions' at all at the other extreme. He declared that he 'made use of Mary'; that she was an element he had always taken into account in making what in the end, he admitted, was his own subjective decision. He saw her as no more dangerous to society than those who took an extreme view dramatically opposed to hers. On the whole, it seems he was trying to perform a job where all the rulebooks had been thrown overboard;

or he was like a man driving through a crowded city where neither he nor anyone else had read the Highway Code. He seemed to me an honest, highly articulate and intelligent man and I was not surprised to learn of his resignation.

Those who know Mary Whitehouse and have followed her career with close attention tend to share Stephen Murphy's opinion that Mary Whitehouse's significance is 'as a phenomenon', rather than as an individual. They feel she was bound to arise in the British Isles eventually because she represents, if a minority view, nevertheless a substantial and sincerely held one. Bill Deedes points out that Mary Whitehouse, for all the sophistication that she has acquired over the past decade has not changed her opinions to any real degree. 'She is still not prepared to compromise. She will never accept any olive branch from anyone, simply for the sake of peace; she will never intellectually split hairs.'

Allegations that she is an instrument of MRA or the CIA are seen by her admirers as the sort of allegations that are bound to be put about by publishers of pornographic material. Although she has not totally destroyed them, she remains a hostile factor, insists Deedes, so some of the ideas disseminated about her have to be taken with a pinch of salt.

Mary Whitehouse's great strength, it appears to those who have studied her closely, is that she does not conform to the accepted standards of debate, as practised, at least, by politicians who appreciate the importance of trimming, of preserving 'a balance' and of not giving hostages to fortune. 'It seems easy to draw up a list of the way her performance might have been improved—that she could have played her cards this way or that or that she should not have jumped down the barrel or reacted to a question as quickly as she did,' said Deedes. But if she had conformed to the smooth practices that distinguish much political debate in Britain, then she would probably have been less effective.

Bill Deedes, for one, tends to disagree with Mary Whitehouse when it comes to the question of distinguishing between what is done in private and what is done in public. Deedes quotes John Stuart Mill's *Essay on Liberty* in which he says that a man should be free to do whatever he wants to do, provided he does not offend his neighbours. This, of course, was the kernel of her argument with the BBC: 'This is why I think Mary Whitehouse has often more justice about what she does about the BBC than the BBC realises. Television after all is a much more difficult medium to control than a porn shop. In porn shops, the material can be kept out of sight so that young children are not liable to be depraved or corrupted. Mill's *dictum* surely stands that whatever adults may wish to see or not wish to see and how ever strongly the State wants to protect that right, its primary duty is to protect young children. 'I feel passionately about this,' declares Deedes. 'As chairman of a Select Committee on Schools and having seen the graffiti written on walls and heard some of the language passing between adolescents these days, I felt that there was a very sharp deterioration in manners not conducive to a civilised society. In a sense, this has been based on imitation and has sprung out of the selfishness of an adult world which has claimed the right to enjoy itself in a rather hedonistic way, has claimed the right to "liberate" sex, to have ideas about sex, to look at sex in any shape or form and has forgotten Mill's very strong reservation that there remains a duty not to corrupt the young.'

Many of her friends believe that by instinct, whichever way she votes at elections, Mary Whitehouse is a conservative ('although that's not an offence for which—as yet—she can be hanged,' says one). Mary is often unselective: there is just as much bad language, both distasteful and sexual, in *Steptoe and Son* as in *Till Death Us Do Part*. It was the radical Left—in itself a small minority group—which wanted a free-for-all in British society with no kinds of restraint, whereas Mary Whitehouse represents much of the broad middle class who in 'an unformed, unshaped, inarticulate way' feel that 'things ought not be allowed to go beyond a certain point.' Bill Deedes, for example, thought it a fair charge that she might be politically prejudiced and that she had attacked programmes for political reasons rather than for strictly anti-pornographic ones. 'But I sense that what she is attacking is not filth, dirt, pornography nor radical ideas—but has been demanding to know *by what right* does the BBC inflict them on the public. She sees the BBC as suffering from a dereliction of its responsibilities and duties rather than denying the existence of certain things or the interest some people have in them.'

Finally, Bill Deedes gives what he considers the irrefutable argument. 'Ask yourself this—suppose you *were* to take Mary Whitehouse out of the public scene—remove her altogether or send her abroad, what corresponding voice of caution would be heard occasionally reminding the BBC that some people were offended by something they had done. In a sense she is an original and she is not always justified in what she does. I know the BBC is sensitive about criticism directed at them—and, in-deed, broadly, they do a superb job. I've come out of politics where plenty of frightfully well-intentioned people, including leaders of parties, believe that they have done their utmost for the public and feel very hurt indeed when people turn round and say they're either unfit for their duties or that they betrayed the nation. But this is the stuff of public life and the Corporation, in particular, must not be too sensitive about some of the things said about them. Even if Mary Whitehouse only gets it right once in ten times—and I think her shooting is probably a bit better than that—in a sense she is doing a public service. After all, no one can say she has actively stopped anything from hap-pening. Johnny Speight is probably right in saying that she has had no *statutory* effect—but on the other hand one cannot be sure how far she has not given a certain amount of courage, of con-viction, of hope to those who feel deeply about these things but who lack the language to express themselves and the guts to put it across. In a free society, it's important that, let's say, even a minority have the feeling that somebody is speaking up for them, is expressing what they want to say—but cannot.'

Mary Whitehouse does not resent the fact that she has been the object of sneers and widespread calumny, remembering that Christ himself had every bit as much to put up with. Yet she takes tremendous satisfaction in the knowledge that her mild and modest little efforts should have snowballed to such importance and in such a fashion. Though she knows she is trying to clean an Augean stable. It is still relatively easy to dismiss her with an indulgent smile, yet there is little doubt that she has had a salu-tary effect on British society—even if it has been only to open the discussion about where the Permissive Society, as far as TV and other public media are concerned, must stop. In this respect, her attitude finds an echo in the words of Sir Michael Swann, the present Chairman of the BBC, in his Earl Grey Memorial lecture at Newcastle in May, 1974. His remarks are illuminating if only for the light they throw on the difficulties inherent in running such an organisation as the BBC—and for the effects of such a body of criticism as provided by Mary Whitehouse.

Sir Michael pointed out that there were those who thought the BBC 'a nest of left-wing subversives working overtime to bring down Conservative Government', indeed many might go farther and suggest that they were out to bring down *all* capital-ist governments, whether conservative or labour. 'And con-versely was it not a different sort of organisation wedded to traditional upper-class capitalist values, working overtime to bring down Labour Governments?' As to violence and sex, it had been agreed that TV had been responsible for 'the supposed decline in our standards'. Yet there were 'plenty of others who see us as a stuffy old Auntie, obsessed with tradition, ritual royal occasions, cosy family situations and much else, being instru-mental therefore in encouraging society to hang on to every out of date notion.' The BBC got contradictory letters 'to the tune of hundreds of thousands a year'.

'An academic, confronted with this sort of Babel,' declared Sir Michael, 'looks at once for reassurance and advice from objective research. But alas, in the world of the mass media, such help is largely wanting. The State maintains Institutes, Laboratories, Centres, Units and groups devoted to the study of heaven knows what, but not to the effects of the mass media, despite the fact that successive governments proclaim these effects to be extensive, important and usually sinister. . . . So I make a plea for some effort being directed towards this neglected area. The broadcasters would welcome it. But . . . the field is uniquely difficult and elusive.' The results of what research already existed, he continued, 'don't add up to very much, as yet'. One or two conclusions did emerge. The setting of televised violence was crucial. Traditional westerns were 'so stylised, the conventions so well understood and so strictly adhered to, that no one, it can be fairly safely assumed, is harmed. Some of the newer westerns, though, are a different story. The horror and suffering of violence is liable to be genuinely portrayed and red blood occasionally spurts from wounds. The whole thing is a lot nearer to reality, even if it is set in the Wild West. *A fortiori*, violence truthfully portrayed, in a modern and familiar setting, is likely to have a profound effect. Even so, quite a lot of evidence suggests that it is not likely to lead its viewers into anti-social action. But, and it is a very serious but, there is now growing evidence that these new realistic sorts of portrayed violence can, and probably do, affect a small fraction of viewers who are in some manner maladjusted, even if they are only a few per cent. I don't believe that the broadcasters—or the film makers—can any longer shrug this off. And to their credit; the broadcasters at least don't try to. But there is a lot of double think on the problem knocking around in society.'

He had deliberately 'trailed his coat and recalled the thalidomide affair. It was not a devilish drug thought up to deform babies but an effective sedative that no doubt did much good. Unfortunately, it was deeply harmful to a small proportion of women who took it. As a result we now have a system whereby drug manufacturers must prove most rigorously that a drug is for all practical purposes harmless to everyone before they are allowed to sell it.

'Why then, I asked, do we not insist on something similar where violence in the media is concerned? The question was directed at the liberal left rather than anywhere else. They after all, were the most vociferous over thalidomide: they are also the most vociferous over total freedom for the media. I never got an answer. No one agreed. No one disagreed. There was what I can only describe as an embarrassed silence. Of course, to prove that a given scene of violence has no ill effects, is not like proving the harmlessness of a drug—though that is difficult enough. And if one must lay down that no violence of any sort was ever to be portrayed unless it could be proved harmless, one would in fact never show anything, even the great classics. But the moral dilemma remains, and I believe the broadcasters and film makers must heed it. The portrayal of violence demands much heart-searching.'

With some justice, Mary Whitehouse now argues along with Sir Michael 'Is it not rather up to us [the BBC] to show that what we screen does not have ill effects, rather than up to others to prove that it does?'

It is only necessary to listen—or even read—Mary Whitehouse's words to realise that she is no ogress. Certainly, so far as her *declared* aims are concerned. There are those who believe in 'Live and let live' who cannot be convinced that she is anything but a fusspot; there are those who say that she is intolerant and should have been satisfied with Mrs Wistrich's defeat without urging an even stiffer censorship. The first is perhaps a typical reaction of much of English society which is often grounded in apathy rather than tolerance, in ignorance of the ramifications of a problem or the desire that it will simply 'go away'. Pornography, permissiveness and violence *are* important issues, whether one feels that society should be more 'open' or whether one believes that things have gone far enough. The second point has considerable force; but I think we should remember that Mrs Whitehouse over the past decade has learned much from her opponents. She has watched them push and push, capping one 'outrage' with an even more daring one. Once somebody draws a line, the forces of permissiveness and anarchy press on until they have pierced it. It is not surprising she decided that her opponents' tactics, which have, so far, brought them immense success, should be turned against them; she has probably also come to appreciate that the best form of defence is attack.

Her present position appears to show the desire to have *official* representation of some sort, for the ordinary viewer, in how television is conducted in this country. She is still astonished at the situation which she found in the BBC when she began probing the workings of the Corporation. There seemed to her to be a chairman and board of governors with a specific duty to the public but who, to her amazement, turned out to be made of cardboard. She was genuinely taken aback to discover, in those early days, that they appeared to have no power—or perhaps no wish to exercise it—to influence the 'level of responsibility' at which programmes were made. She still sees the weakness of the system in the freedom allowed to individual producers and those who actually *create* the programmes, the writers and artists whose talents are hired by the Corporation.

'Once the fact of the medium's power to influence be accepted then the vital question becomes—what is its message *in toto*? What does it say about human relations, about the family, the home and about men and women? The truth of the matter is that broadcasting has a wealth of internal patronage which enables producers, commentators and playwrights to swing the thinking of millions behind their own particular political, cultural and ethical loyalties. . . . Until we devise better means of governing this explosive influence over the human mind then inevitably demand for control—and political control at that—

will grow stronger. Our quest must be to find a right system of government for this new manifestation of power before the politicians get in on the act. . . . The freedom of the professional has to be balanced against the right of the individual to maintain certain standards within his own home, to sit and view without having to accept gratuitous indecency and foul language as an integral part of the evening's entertainment. . . . The only acceptable alternative to dictatorship either from within or without the medium is an informed and involved populace. Democracy must be made to work within broadcasting as elsewhere. The responsibility must be accepted as "ours" rather than "theirs". A generation must be trained which has enough understanding of the medium of broadcasting to criticise both objectively and intelligently. Fear and frustration will, to a great extent, be answered by education and knowledge. Changes must be initiated which will enable the viewer and listener to feel that he is important, that his voice is listened to, that his ideas are valid, that his experience is of value. Steps must be taken to ensure that dialogue between both sides of the screen becomes a reality. . . . The rights of the viewer to a voice in the discussion about standards and policies must be translated into practicalities. In Britain we have advisory councils appointed by the broadcasting authorities themselves: councils which give no account of their stewards to the public on whose behalf they advise. These should be replaced by totally independent councils able to report back and meet with the viewer at regular intervals.

'Ministerial broadcasts are a regular feature of our television screen. We would like to see the Chairman of the BBC and of the Independent Broadcasting Authority on the screen, too, giving an account of their stewardship, an outline of policies, an account of changing priorities. Communication is what broadcasting is all about. Two-way communication would not only solve many of the problems which bedevil the industry's public relations, it would open up whole new spheres of creative activity.'

The skill of the woman, her sure grasp of how the power strings are manipulated in modern society, has perhaps never been shown better than in the last paragraph of this statement. At a time when the left wing in Britain has brought massive pressure against the existing structure of industrial management; when Tony Benn's new Bill seeks to provide a statutory obligation on all companies to run their businesses only with the advice and consent of their work force, Mrs Whitehouse demands that *viewers* must be consulted about what is or what is not put on their TV screen. She is surely stealing the Emperor's clothes.

And yet, it will be argued, how can she ever hope to curb successfully TV, cinema or stage performances which, in the last analysis, depend on the writers and producers. Can artists be forced to conform to rules; reporters to report only what is palatable? Where does liberty degenerate into licence; when is dictatorship the only valid answer to licence? Or as Pilate asked, what is truth? Or perhaps the question is, do we want it?

Mary Whitehouse, looking out at the Clee Hills, hazy and bluish, says that the most marvellous thing about her life at present is that she never knows where it will lead her next. She has no plans for her own life: 'I live in the present and am not concerned with the past or with the future—except in as much as what we do today can affect our children's lives for good or ill.'

She admits to little interest in party political matters *per se*. 'We sent out a questionnaire on the Indecent Displays Bill to both Conservative and Labour parties—and what was interesting was that almost without exception the Tories said they were against indecent displays while Labour was not prepared to stop them. In this instance, therefore, we, as an association would be against Labour.' But when the Labour party attacked the BBC for alleged bias during the 1974 general election, Mary Whitehouse, to the astonishment of many who do not understand her reasoning, at once rushed to the Corporation's defence. 'It is difficult to evade the conclusion that the real motive behind the complaint is the establishment of a platform from which moves for the political control of broadcasting could be launched. We regard this as highly dangerous and have assured Sir Michael (Swann) of our fullest support.'

She has no nostalgia for the British Empire; she is not worried about hordes of foreigners in Britain as is her former neighbour, Enoch Powell. She believes in the right of the Third World nations to achieve independence and wholly favours it but says: 'Don't expect me to pronounce upon each individual case—I simply don't know enough about the subject. In principle, I'm in favour of all these freedom movements in Africa and South America, but the problem is to distinguish which is a genuine and spontaneous desire for liberty and which movement is simply a front for Communism.' Communist infiltration is still a matter which pre-occupies her: 'They've infiltrated the trade unions. Why does anyone still believe they haven't infiltrated broadcasting?'

Mary Whitehouse is truly passionate about her convictions; yet she sits in 'the snug' and declares her strongest held beliefs in a totally unimpassioned tone; one remembers that she was a school mistress. She allows you to make a point and only when she is satisfied that it has been stated and that she has digested all its implications, does she reply; she is cool, relaxed and one can almost hear the wheels of her brain whirling; she lacks entirely any quality of demagoguery. She is no La Passionara. But she is prepared to outline what she too has been striving for:

'Ideally, for me, English society would be a Christian one— but what I've never said is that people who are not Christian should be prevented from having their say. The kind of society I want is one which will allow me to go on preaching my views— that is all. What I'm concerned about is *freedom*. I'm certainly the leader of a pressure group on the sex problem—but that comes down in the end to our responsibility to protect the youth of the country. I look around and see young people being grossly exploited—often for no other reason than a commercial motive.

My protest—our protest as an association—is *not* a negative thing; it is a positive attempt to free children from exploitation.

'I think it's often forgotten that in this country—and nobody would deny that we're all football mad—that more people still attend church on Sunday than go to football matches; oh, I know, you'd never think it from television! And here's another statistic—when people are asked if they want their children brought up in the Christian ethic, 95 per cent of parents always answer "yes". I think the Church *is* in disarray—and I believe TV is largely responsible for it. Throughout history, certainly, there have been always new ideas—radical ideas. The difference today is that people are now exposed to the most powerful medium ever invented; a medium that makes an impact out of all proportion to what it is actually saying and it is now far more easy to confuse people. It is the *proportions* that are all wrong.

'This brings me back to my original point. When I speak, there is an immediate outcry about "censorship". But a form of censorship has been going on in this country for the past twenty years; suppose you have four people on a discussion panel and one of them is a Communist—well, that's out of proportion. It's a form of censorship in itself—and I have always believed that unless people speak out and declare that this or that is an offence against their standards of decency or values, then how are the broadcasting authorities to know where to draw the line? That is why it has been necessary to speak up.'

CHAPTER ELEVEN

How National VALA Works

By the last week of March 1975, Mary Whitehouse was a little tired, a little strained, even a little apprehensive—but clearly still as indomitable as ever.

She had never been a hundred per cent fit since she caught malaria on a visit to Gambia in 1973. Now, at the end of a long and hard 'season' commencing in October and including her rousing battle with Mrs Enid Wistrich of the Greater London Council over the abolition of film censorship and National VALA's annual convention in the Midland Hotel, Birmingham (addressed by Sir Keith Joseph) in February, she had come—temporarily—to the end of her physical resources.

One thing was spilling over into another. Book reviews, articles for the *Sunday Times* and *Church Times*; presentation of National VALA's award to the *Softly, Softly* team (February 26); helping son Christopher edit and collate *The Viewer and Listener*; researching material for the Townswomen's Guilds with which to fight proposals for lowering the age of consent to fourteen and issuing contraceptives on the National Health; plus her usual work as hon. general secretary—and miles and miles of travel.

A week in mid-March was not altogether atypical. Work all day Monday dealing with the multifarious matters relating to National VALA. That evening a drive of fifty miles to address a meeting; next day to Sheffield, to debate with permissive publisher John Calder at the University; a night in a Sheffield hotel, then down to London to appear on the BBC's *Woman's Hour*; a long lie-in on Thursday morning before a tiring drive to Merthyr Tydfil in south Wales to speak at a Methodist church meeting.

Before she could get away from the Wyre Forest, however, the BBC were on the telephone. Would she do a radio show? Would she do a TV show? Where? Cardiff. OK. So Ernest turned the prow of the little light mustard-coloured DAF automatic in the direction of the Welsh capital where she spent a tiring afternoon before driving on to Merthyr.

Merthyr proved a huge success. But next morning, the BBC wanted her once again. Back down to Cardiff therefore for a half-hour recorded discussion on censorship for BBC TV, Wales. On the way home, a stop for lunch someplace where she remembers being taken 'poorly'. Ernest bundled her into the DAF and she recalled nothing more until she woke up in her own bed at home.

She really ought to have taken it a bit more easy at that stage. But on the Monday she was due to address the Dudley College of Education and on Tuesday to deliver a speech in London— two long-standing appointments which she had already been forced to cancel once. Rather than disappoint her hosts again and although still feeling utterly wretched, Mary gamely carried through with her programme. She arrived home from London at 9 o'clock that night, once again prostrate.

It was at this critical juncture that a woman reporter from a jazzy Fleet Street newspaper chose to request an interview. A day or so later, Mary Whitehouse faced a formidable battery of questions. The interrogation was clearly aimed—validly enough, of course—at cutting her down to size. Which meant, in effect, suggesting that Mary Whitehouse was a *papier maché* figure; that National VALA was more or less a fraud; that when she opened her mouth and spoke, Mary Whitehouse was doing nothing more than giving vent to her own prejudices. As Mrs Whitehouse not altogether cheerfully admits, 'I wasn't at my best'.

The interview, in fact, highlighted nothing very new. It brought out such familiar facts as that Mary and Ernest tend to spend most of their days in autumn and winter in 'the snug', heaping massive blocks of wood on to a roaring fire in whose

inglenook shelf rests a coloured photograph of Mary talking to
the Pope. Nor was the main question raised—exactly what body
of opinion in Britain did Mary Whitehouse represent and how
many citizens subscribed to her views?—entirely unfamiliar.
The approach was reminiscent of the days when her keenest
critics could dismiss her as an obscurantist figure from the wilds
of darkest Worcestershire. And as such, it ran off Mary Whitehouse more or less like the proverbial water off the proverbial
duck's back.

As is usual with the majority of her critics, the reporter handed
a great deal to Mary on a plate. Take that play *Leeds United* by
the ex-*Z Cars* star, Colin Welland, which occupied two hours of
BBC TV time on October 31, 1973. Now, didn't Mary Whitehouse realise that she had 'made a lot of people' angry by her
criticisms? For someone whose principal purpose was to show up
Mary Whitehouse as a one-woman band who spoke for an insignificant fraction of the British people, this was a magnificent
example of how to lead with your chin. Exactly how many
people had been 'made angry' by Mrs W's criticism? And what
fraction of the British public did *they* represent? In the absence
of another national referendum we shall, of course, never know.
But it was yet another example of the sloppy, ill-considered and
rather ill-judged attempts by her opponents to discredit a figure
who might well have been at one time open to the charge of
obscurantism—and who might still have to yield some ground
before an expertly conducted demolition job.

Now exactly what was it about *Leeds United* that Mary Whitehouse objected to—apart from the enormous expense which the
play involved? First, it seemed, there was the bad language;
second, 'it was a piece of propaganda'. And political propaganda,
Mrs W. pointed out, was not the function of the publicly supported broadcasting service called the BBC.

Mrs Whitehouse, of course, had her ground fairly solidly prepared. After the transmission of the 'play', the *Yorkshire Evening
Post* had run a symposium under the heading 'Was this how it

was?'. The bulk of the letters insisted that Welland's version of affairs was a travesty of the truth. What annoyed many of those who wrote and who had also taken part in the strike was the gratuitous bad language they were alleged to have used. Mary added that her principal objection to the play—apart from the language and the expense—was the fact that the average BBC viewer was left unaware that he had been manipulated, been subjected to political indoctrination. 'It's important that viewers should know the motivation', she insisted.

None of this, of course, was quite what the reporter had hoped for. She demanded to know if Mrs W. would have objected had the political sympathies of the writer and producer been announced and seemed rather surprised when Mrs W. declared that that was exactly what she wanted. 'The important thing is to know who is putting it out.' In fact, since the transmission date, Mrs Whitehouse had been doing some quiet digging of her own into the backgrounds of the writer and producer and the spring issue of *Viewer and Listener* for 1975 carried the following item:

On 31 October 1974 the BBC televised a film called 'Leeds United' which purported to give a factual account of the strike of women clothing workers in Leeds. On the following day the Leftwing journal *Workers' Press* carried a report of the film by a 'guest reviewer' who said that: 'The film's analysis was consistent with Workers' Press own political assessment of the Leeds strike as reported in the winter of 1969–70.' The reviewer also commented that the film reflected 'a new stage in the class struggle'.

This is hardly surprising since it was directed by Mr Roy Battersby, who is a Central Committee member of the Workers' Revolutionary Party, and written by Mr Colin Welland, who was one of the sponsors of the 'Road to Workers' Power Pageant' held at the Empire Pool, Wembley, in March, 1974.

The reporter was actually on to rather hotter stuff, in a sense, when she quizzed Mary, not so much about the bases of her 'protests', as about the methods she employed. Were an enemy to set out to explode the 'myth' of Mary Whitehouse, they would be bound to discover that her Achilles heel was more likely to embrace National VALA and her relationship to it, than the sense or commonsense of her arguments. To do the reporter justice, she did try to probe this weakness. How did Mary decide when to complain and what about? Did she wait until the members wrote or telephoned her? Or did she just lift the telephone and lodge a complaint off her own bat? These were pretty fast balls and Mary Whitehouse, like an England opening batsman, cautiously hints that her stumps were for a little while in some danger.

National VALA can, in fact, boast of no more than 31,000 subscribing members. In that sense, it consists of a relatively insignificant proportion of the British population. On the other hand, it is doubtful if the British Trotskyist party numbers more —and it is also probably true that neither Mr Welland nor Mr Battersby would claim that they were speaking for others than themselves. To the objective mind, therefore the right of Mr Welland or Mr Battersby to inflict their idiosyncratic views on a large segment of the British population is no stronger than Mrs Whitehouse's right to dissent; in fact she might argue that, in general, she spoke for more people.

A calm—and perhaps sympathetic—look at Mary's dilemma might show that very often she has no other recourse than to speak out off her own bat. National VALA is not a highly organised, highly paid professional group of people. They consist so far as anyone can judge from addresses, the spelling and punctuation of their letters and their (sometimes) professed qualifications, of a random cross-section of the citizenship. One thing is certain: if Mary Whitehouse set out to canvass the opinion of every single member of the Association about every single programme she considered objectionable, she would find herself in a position not dissimilar to Mr Harold Wilson if he had to hold a national referendum every time he decided to light his pipe.

First of all, by the very nature of her appointment—and her position has to be re-affirmed annually at the convention—she is the chosen spokeswoman of the organisation. Under the rules, she is empowered to answer the queries of newspapers. And on the whole, she insists, the bulk of her so-called 'protests' arise out of phone calls *from* newspapers or other branches of the media. On more significant issues, she first talks to as many members of the Executive Committee of National VALA (six officers headed by Mr John Barnett, former Chief Constable of Lincolnshire and President of the Association—and eleven Committee members who stand down every two years) as are readily available and who may have seen the programme. Sometimes, though, the objections *have* to be made on a more or less hit-or-miss basis. Normally, except where she is absolutely sure of her ground, however, she will try and take counsel. But she is guided by the constitution of National VALA; by the knowledge that she has been the inspiration, driving force and founder of the Association; by the flood of information and opinion that constantly funnels into her office. She is the spearhead of the organisation and would never deny it; yet she has made whatever efforts she can to see that her 'baby' is as democratically based and operated as is feasible, always allowing for the fact that it is an entirely voluntary body.

She displays a discreet awareness that this can threaten to be a weakness on her position; it is a weakness that all those she thinks of as her enemies and opponents have never hesitated to exploit. Partly to this end, partly to make sure that the leadership was not getting out of step with the membership, partly to aid the membership to express their views, Mary had 15,000 research cards despatched to the VALA membership in October, 1974. Six months later, over 3,000 members had expressed opinions—and more cards were still trickling in daily.

A random sample in no way suggests that National VALA members are any more intolerant or unreasonable than might be expected. Of *Spring and Port Wine*: 'Entertaining and full of human interest. Congratulations to author, actors, and producer.' Of *Jane Eyre*: 'A beautiful production. Very well worth watching even though repeated rather soon. An oasis in the desert of Saturday evening's programmes.' Of *Dixon of Dock Green*: 'Had looked forward to return of this series but found it disappointing. No human interest. Characters were puppets and story unconvincing.' Of *School for Scandal*: 'Well produced. Altogether very much enjoyed.' Of *The World About Us* 'A delightful programme. Thank you, BBC2.' Of *Newsday*: 'This feature is a very good one.' Of the *Missiles of October*: 'It was an excellent production.' Not all, of course, were quite so appreciative. Of a schools programme at that time: 'Ostensibly moral (sic!) education, the covert "indoctrination" of philistine attitudes by cleverly worded innuendoes has to be seen to be believed.' Of *A Small Imperfection*: 'A programme on spina bifida children, the general tone of which was "better they should not live". Ended up showing 18-month-old baby-girl whose parents had agreed to allow it to die a natural death— in a few weeks time—very heavily loaded towards euthanasia— very emotive.' Others objected to the use of words like "bloody" and "arse" in programmes and to nudity in an episode of *The Love School*—because it seemed 'quite unnecessary'. On the whole, the batch of replies failed to disclose any particularly dim-witted views—and while one might personally disagree or agree with the views expressed—they did seem to indicate that the correspondents did not only treat television as moving wall paper but were pretty alert and involved in what they saw.

It has to be said, nevertheless, that Mary Whitehouse remained slightly apprehensive about the outcome of the interview. The paper concerned had a reputation for sizzling sensationalism linked to nude pin-ups. The reporter herself was well known among her Fleet Street colleagues as holding pretty extreme views and principles. The combination of an editorial policy based on sensation and excitement plus an inquirer whom Mary feared might be prepared to label her as 'reactionary' boded little good. And in the event, the 'tone' of the article did little to dispel her fears. How many Britons did Mary Whitehouse really speak for? screamed the headline—and invited its readers to tell them the answer.

The newspaper in question was hardly one likely to circulate widely among 'middle-class' households. The advertising marketing men divide newspaper readership into A, B, C, D and E categories—A and B representing those, allegedly, with the higher educational, intellectual and professional back-grounds, the rest—largely—embracing those working in the manual fields. On the whole, this newspaper's readership was largely made up of the C, D and E categories—many of them obviously trade unionists and probably supporters of the Labour Party. Although these conclusions are merely suppositions, they are based on an informed guess.

On the evidence of her own experiences while addressing meetings up and down the country, Mary Whitehouse had little doubt that the views she expressed reflected the opinions of many more than the subscribing members of National VALA. Apathy, after all, was a besetting fault of the British people. The national tendency was 'not to bother', to shrug the shoulders, to leave the job to someone else. By nature, too, not everyone was 'a joiner'; nor did everyone wanted to fork out a subscription, however modest. Nonetheless, the odds seemed rather loaded against her.

It would be wrong to suggest that she ever missed a wink of sleep over the matter. But nevertheless, as spring-like March gave way to a wintry April, Mary Whitehouse, still rather exhausted, could not conceal her mild apprehension. The interview had not been one of her best performances; here and there she may have sold the pass a little. Would her temporary *gaucherie* have tipped the scale?

In the event, she won a minor triumph. The readership,

admitted the newspaper, was split about fifty-fifty on the issue. But of the twelve letters they printed, no fewer than seven favoured Mary Whitehouse and her campaign; five were against. A mother of four wrote: 'I feel a great debt of gratitude to Mrs Whitehouse for all her hard work and unfailing good humour in the face of much ridicule. She says and stands for what we believe and know to be the truth in our hearts but are either too lazy or too timid to say ourselves.' A male reader coined the slogan, 'Carry on, Mrs Whitehouse!'

It would be fair to say that Mary Whitehouse felt herself vindicated.

CHAPTER TWELVE

Censorship and Liberty

There were big issues, medium-sized issues and what a Fleet Street sub-editor in one of his less rapturous moments might call piddling issues. Big, less-big, tiny?—who was to judge? Were they actually Whitehouse campaigns or merely media echoes of what Mrs Whitehouse and her confrères might be expected to feel? As Mary Whitehouse likes to point out, at least eight out of every ten times her name appears in the newspapers, it has been as the result of a gratuitous reference to her by someone else; and on at least four out of those eight occasions, the writers invariably attribute to her views she doesn't even hold. Even when she does say something, it will not necessarily be reported accurately or within its context.

There was *Dr Who* for instance. *Dr Who*, for those who might well ask who *Dr Who* is, is a BBC children's programme which is slotted in somewhere just after the Saturday sports results and shortly before the Saturday Night movie or the current pop-singer which the BBC wiseacres, by some mad phantasmagoric delusion, desperately conceive to be 'entertainment'. On the whole, *Dr Who* isn't a programme the BBC has any need to be defensive about. It was certainly not, so far as the majority of the citizens of the sceptred isle are concerned, high on the list of their controversial priorities. Nonetheless, according to the newspapers one day, Mary Whitehouse was suddenly against it. On the whole, the puzzled reaction might be reasonably interpreted as What! is nothing sacred? Or even, what next?

Mrs Whitehouse, in fact, had not exactly taken up her

cudgels and deliberately decided to flail poor *Dr Who*. In January 1975, she was attending an international broadcasting seminar held at Manchester University where the telecommunications people solemnly discussed *Dr Who*. It is easy to be flippant, of course; in fact, the question of what is implanted on the impressionable minds of young British children is the keynote of much that Mrs Whitehouse struggled for. She is only too aware that the future pattern and structure of the country depends on what today's young minds see and hear. Shaun Sutton, head of BBC TV drama, said that the Corporation had never carried out any research on the effect of their programmes —and in particular, *Dr Who*—on children under five. Mrs Whitehouse pointed out that from research carried out by National VALA and from the opinions expressed to her by parents at various meetings she had addressed, there was some concern about the programme and the effect it might have on tiny tots. Even children aged two or three were not generally packed off to bed as early as 5.30. Would the BBC at least not consider putting the programme back to 6.30 when the very young ones were out of harm's way?

It was this remark that led one newspaper to headline a squib the following day: 'Mrs W. slaps an X certificate on *Dr Who*.' As Mrs W. points out, 'You do, in fact, get terrifying, horrific creatures pictured on *Dr Who*. No one at the BBC, apparently, stops to consider the impact of such sights on little children who are incapable of rationalising what's on the box. And the programme—and I understand the dramatic need to do so, of course—always stops at a point of tension. So you have these tiny tots suffering tension for a whole week before the next episode is shown. *That's* what I was talking about. Not that there isn't violence and sadism in the programme. The episode screened on Saturday, March 22, had more violence than I can remember—and at times it was really sadistic; indeed such was the level of violence that I believe this particular episode should not have been screened before 9 pm. It is difficult to imagine the effect it must have had on any pliable mind under the age of fourteen.'

In Mrs Whitehouse's mind, the issue of *Dr Who* is really no less important than the two great *causes célèbres* which marked her activities of the early seventies: the controversy over the films *Blow Out* and *Deep Throat* and her extraordinary intervention and personal duel with Mrs Enid Wistrich, chairman of the GLC's Film Viewing Board, over the abolition of censorship in London. They are all segments of a mosaic; a mosaic which in turn, forms no more than a segment of an even larger mosaic.

To Mrs Whitehouse's way of thinking, modern communications are interlaced. Books, magazines, newspapers, radio, television, films, whether they lean towards education or mere 'entertainment', are methods of informing or swaying individual judgement. On the whole, her commitment is to broadcasting which, because of television, has now supplanted the others as the single greatest mass influence. She is not a filmgoer but as the old cosy films of the thirties, forties and early fifties with their inflexible codes of behaviour gave way to the more 'permissive' productions of the sixties and seventies, she became aware that British television screens were increasingly filled by material which according to her standards was lamentable. She was not slow, either, to note that within five years (films are normally not shown on TV until they are at least five years old), there was nothing to stop the BBC or IBA transmitting the increasingly 'shocking' material which had begun to find its way into the commercial cinemas.

Her sources and contacts in the United States (where she had travelled widely a few years before) had told her about *Deep Throat*. Soho film entrepreneurs, such as a man called James Vaughan who are not, seemingly, so much concerned with the artistic value of films as their viability at the box office, were hopeful that *Deep Throat*, whose theme deals with oral sex, would be among the box office winners of 1973. When Mary

Whitehouse read in the press that Vaughan was hoping to import *Deep Throat* for public showing—and that within five years it stood a good chance of creeping into a BBC TV programme—she travelled down to London and bearded the chiefs of the Customs and Excise in their den. As a result—or so she claims—although copies of *Deep Throat* are lying about in scruffy Soho rooms and may even be now and then shown privately in clubs, the Customs and Excise have warned people like Vaughan and other impresarios of a like mind that any attempt to show the film publicly will result in its confiscation.

She was less fortunate with *Blow Out* and, as a result, now argues that because of inadequate law and the pusillanimous attitude of the Director of Public Prosecutions office (which she believes to be staffed with too many 'permissively' minded individuals) there is nothing other than the Customs and Excise standing between the great British public and a Denmark-type state of affairs.

Blow Out certainly attempted new artistic standards—at least in those hitherto neglected fields of gluttony and masturbation. *Blow Out* has a middle-aged man being masturbated by his elderly nurse; a woman attempting sexual intercourse with a motor exhaust pipe; the act of anal intercourse and a man having food shovelled down his throat while a woman masturbates him until he dies. It was not really the sort of film the British Board of Film Censors and its then secretary, Stephen Murphy, with their innate desire to please everybody, felt could be passed for public exhibition. Under the guidance of Mrs Wistrich, however, the GLC took a more lenient view and the film was duly screened at the Curzon Cinema in Mayfair, a distinguished theatre which has consistently screened most of the best films ever made. It is true, of course, that by virtue of its prices and, so to speak, its editorial policy, it is a haven of elitism. Very few members of the trade union or manual classes ever tread its sacred carpets; muddied oafs, on the whole, would find themselves out of place.

But what of the law, Mrs Whitehouse wondered? Accompanied by two male members of the Executive Committee of National VALA, Mrs Whitehouse went to see the film and, after the showing, dashed off to the nearest police station to lodge a complaint. There she learned that other members of the public had also tried to have the film stopped but the police had explained that there was no law on the subject; or what law there was, was too insubstantial to cope. In due course, the volume of complaints developed into such a crescendo that the DPP's office was asked to arbitrate but eventually declined to take action.

'We then felt that the best thing to do was to test the law in Court ourselves,' says Mrs Whitehouse. 'Unfortunately the only law we could find that *might* prove applicable was a prosecution under the Vagrancy Act. Everything turned upon the question of whether a cinema is a public place or not.' On April 8 1974, Mrs Whitehouse's private prosecution was heard by Mr Evelyn Russell, the magistrate, at Bow Street. Mark Potter QC represented Mrs Whitehouse and Richard du Cann QC, brother of the Tory politician and financier, represented the management of the cinema.

A Fleet Street woman columnist was later to write; 'I suddenly felt sorry for Mary Whitehouse. . . . I don't always agree with what she does. Too often she makes a mountain of principle out of a molehill of bad taste, too often takes a hammer to crack an unimportant nut. But last week when she brought a private summons, I thought she was the bravest woman in the world. She had to come to court and state exactly what she found offensive about the film, had to outline in full the sequences she found particularly disgusting. It must have been a humiliating experience, enough to make the average woman cringe with embarrassment. She may be contrary Mary at times but you cannot deny her courage, she's not afraid to stand up and be counted. She's not afraid of being laughed at, not afraid of going against the trend, not afraid to carry the can

for her convictions. It's one thing to sound off in print, quite
another to get into the ring and do the fighting. . . .'

Mary Whitehouse gratefully accepts the compliment but
declares that the piece itself bears the stamp of journalistic
licence. According to her own diary she 'Went straight to Bow
Street—place full of photographers. Case lasted over two hours.
I was in witness box for about twenty minutes. I must say that
Mr Du Cann is not a particularly attractive type. He gave a long
pause between each of his questions—I suppose to disconcert me.
And he would look over my head. I answered most of them yes
or no and when I ventured to enlarge on one, he came back
quite sharply "I was just about to ask you that, Mrs Whitehouse". Mark Potter suggested he would describe the film and
that I would not need to be called but I begged to disagree,
since it was important that the nature of the film should be
known to justify the summons. And while I knew the press
mightn't pick up what he said about the film, they'd pick up
what I said. Du Cann did not concentrate on defending the
film, which I would have thought impossible, but on calling the
charge "mischievous" and dismissing it as "untenable". He
concentrated on trying to prove that the cinema was not a
public place. At the end the magistrate said he would need time
to consider all the legal points and the case was adjourned until
April 26.'

In seeking to recollect exactly what occurred on the adjourn-
ment, Mrs Whitehouse has to leaf through the pages of her
celebrated diary and suddenly her word springs vividly to life as
she reads out the day by day entries in her rather flat Cheshire
accent. She's away for a holiday with friends in Italy and has
her hair done on the way to the station. Again she's on her way
to Norwich where she does an interview for Anglia TV excoriat-
ing both TV channels for devoting hours and hours to the
soccer World Cup at *the same time*. She addresses a meeting of
350 people that evening; addresses another bunch at lunch the
following day and yet another meeting the following night. On

April 25, she is reading 'a good piece' about herself in the local Anglian newspaper as the train scuds her to London's Liverpool Street where she spends the night before travelling the following morning to Brighton for lunch with a professor before addressing, on the subject of mental pollution, the full congress of 1,500 members of the Royal Society of Health. The meeting proves rather stormy, several members objecting to her being invited to speak but others come to her aid with a burst of slow-hand-clapping and a stamping of feet. An interview for Brighton radio is followed by a train trip to Southampton where she spends the night preparing for an early broadcast on radio Solent at 9 a.m.

Thence to London and to Bow Street for the magistrate's decision. Mr Russell there described her as a 'sincere and courageous woman'. He added, 'so many of us hear things which are offensive in public and merely shrug our shoulders'. Unfortunately, although in his view *Blow Out* was an indecent exhibition, there was no offence under the Vagrancy Act because the Curzon Cinema was not a public place within the meaning of the Act. Interviewed by the press after the decision, Mrs Whitehouse declared that 'if the Customs and Excise had done their job, there would have been no need for me to have brought this prosecution. As it is, it exposes the inadequacy of the law, which needs to be changed'.

She had lost the case but she still feels that she had won the battle. She now says, 'That put the lid on *Deep Throat*, anyway. The Customs, however, said that it was too late to do anything about *Blow Out*—which was unfortunate.'

One battle was over. But the war was still on.

For Londoners, it was an unusual spectacle. Everybody, by now, was pretty well fed up with demos. Never a week-end passed, it seemed, without a long straggling line of scruffy protesters marching to demand that somebody somewhere remedied their grievances. On the evidence of the demos alone, it seemed clear that the British were among the most discontented lot on earth and that that well-known prison camp, Soviet Russia, was a snow-covered Costa Brava by comparison.

Tuesday, January 28 1975 had at least two distinctive qualities about the demo held that day. First, nobody was actually on strike and second, nobody was after more money. There were other differences. Demos were invariably week-end affairs—yet this was a Tuesday. Again, those professional agitators whose faces had become so familiar to the Metropolitan Police were absent. What was pretty unusual about this bunch, too, was that they appeared to be praying from time to time— that is, when they weren't singing a pre-rock version of music that some people actually recognised as hymns.

History of a sort—as it has always been—was once again being made beside the River Thames. The Greater London Council, guider of the destinies of almost ten million Britons, was meeting to decide upon an issue which cut right across traditional party lines. Was the report prepared by Mrs Enid Wistrich, chairman of their Film board, advocating the abolition of film censorship in London, going to be adopted? If Mrs Wistrich's view prevailed, then the views of the British Board of Film Censors could be flouted—and the town was wide open. To some, it held out the promise that from now on, anything could go.

On the surface, the issue seemed an odd one. Inherent in us all, I suppose, there is the unshakeable notion that nobody has the right to make up our minds for us about anything. We feel we have an inalienable right to believe, for instance, in God— or not: just as we choose. To get drunk if we wish; to sing; to kiss a girl; climb a mountain—there are no limits to our private world and its inalienable rights. On the other hand, we soon learn that most of our rights are not supreme. We have no prescriptive right to take a trip round the world—unless we can earn the money to pay for it. We cannot walk across the Sahara desert—because the sun and lack of water soon put a stop to that idea. We cannot make love to that woman—because to begin with she doesn't like us and anyway she's married. We cannot drive down Western Avenue at 100 mph in a Mini—partly because the car won't go that fast and partly because the police would arrest us if we did. We can't even avoid paying income tax. To a modern man, enmeshed in an urban society, the only free souls left in the world appear to be the bedouin of Arabia, the Indians of South America, the Esquimo of the Arctic and the tinkers of Ireland. Patrick Henry had obviously got it all wrong for now we have neither liberty nor death. All our acts are at once circumscribed by the need to take somebody's else's rights or convenience into consideration. Urban society, we soon discover, has imposed its own censorship—just as life itself has forbidden us to do without food and shelter, without sun and rain. Wherever we move, somebody has drawn a chalk line over which we step at our peril. If, on the other hand, we all step over everybody's else's line, then the result is anarchy; as in parts of Belfast. Civilisation, we find, simply means having due regard for the other fellow's chalk line. The options are between civilisation—even at the risk of a *pax romana*—and a jolly jungle where the devil takes the hindmost and the man with the biggest cudgel takes all. Which, at first sight, may seem a long way from the notion of censorship. But as soon as we expose any modern society to the microscope, we find that some form of censorship —in the sense of a willingness to forgo some of our inalienable rights in the interests of the whole community—is inherent in the system.

The idea of censorship is abhorrent, nonetheless—and although it operates in almost every activity we undertake, we are inclined to feel that the less there is of it, the more freedom we would enjoy. Yet, just as one man's wage increase is another man's price rise, if an individual's freedom is extended it can mean that another man's liberty is eroded. On the whole, censorship is part of the balancing act which enables most of us to go about our daily business without being mugged, murdered, raped or robbed. Civilisation, in short, is a delicate balance of checks and counter-checks. What would appear to function best is a system where extremism is only allowed sparingly. Too often, it appears to stand for bigotry and intolerance, dogmatism and persecution. If you're not with me, *ipso facto*, you're against me.

Perhaps the best and most readily understood form of 'censorship' today is that ordinance which forbids driving faster than 30 mph in a built-up area. It is an intolerable interference with liberty. Often it appears so unnecessary. Many decent drivers could happily career through the streets of our cities (if traffic conditions permitted) at 60 mph and would rarely, if ever, collide with a lorry or knock down and kill a three-year old child. Everybody *knows* this. Yet the appalling statistics are there. There are lunatics, it appears, who cannot drive to begin with; who get inordinately drunk; who fall asleep at the wheel—who do a myriad things they shouldn't and who end up killing or maiming themselves (which may not be altogether a bad thing) and much worse, clouting some other innocent often fatally.

In a society where violent thuggery has not been eliminated; where robbery, rape, stealing, brutality *ad nauseam* continue to flourish; where millions of pounds are spent on efforts to educate and reform and deter, the idea that *all* forms of censorship should be abandoned may well appear *outré*. It sits with the idea that as the road toll mounts, all speed limits should be abandoned and all penalties for dangerous driving, drunken driving and so on, jettisoned. Some will still drive dangerously, some will still drive drunkenly—the road casualties will mount; but as all this happens, does the argument for abolishing all control thereby lose force?

In a sense this is what censorship is all about. Is it right to call a halt at some point, however far along the road? Or is it better to allow unfettered liberty perhaps leading to a society which can enjoy both liberty *and* death?

Mrs Whitehouse makes no bones about it; she wants censorship.

It is the kernel, she says, of all her campaigns. She qualifies her demand, of course. She is point-blank against any form of political censorship, but feels that the Broadcasting Authorities should label all material which is 'political propaganda.' Indeed, she would argue, the very failure of the BBC or IBA to label material pro-Trotskyist, pro-Flatearther, pro-Conservative Party, pro-Zionist, pro-American, is in itself a form of political censorship. The people of Britain are being censored from knowing the truth, which, in her opinion, is different from allowing the promulgation of material that may appeal to the worst instincts in human nature. And to deny that people *have* bad instincts is to countenance the Stalinist concentration camps, the excesses of the capitalist industrialists and the extermination of millions of Polish Catholics, Russian atheists and Jews, either by malice or default, by the Nazis of Germany. She insists that the concepts of good and evil are not abstractions; they are no more open to argument than night and day.

But it is clear that there are groups who are opposed to all censorship—that is, of a moral or sociological nature. Mrs Whitehouse sees four strands of interest at work in the censorship debate. The first two debate the issue on the question of 'liberty'. The second two do not; of the latter, there are the pornographers who are simply out to profit from a growing industry and to encourage the growth of that industry whether it harms anybody or not; and there are the revolutionaries— American Jerry Rubin with his 'Do it in the streets' syndrome and that now almost-forgotten figure, Richard Neville, with his declaration that the weapons of revolution are 'obscenity, blasphemy and drugs'. On the whole, the revolutionaries and the pornographer pedlars are no less insidious in her eyes than the libertarians, but they are easier to handle because their behaviour and methods are so blatantly counter-productive. On the other hand, the cry of 'liberty' has a good old-fashioned ring about it and there is a feeling that all good men and true should rally around the flag.

Those concerned with liberty, therefore, divide into two
camps. One believes that a line must be drawn somewhere and
the other doesn't think it at all necessary. The second, Mrs
Whitehouse believes, and cites Mrs Wistrich as an example,
asserts that the 'rights of the individual are paramount and pays
little heed to the possibility of the moral, or indeed, physical,
harm that the "rights" of some individuals may cause in the
lives of others.' The first—in which category she includes herself, sees the 'individual as part of a society in which responsibilities as well as rights and privileges exist'.

On the evidence of this kind of argument, Mrs Whitehouse
really does demolish most of the shafts of ridicule and allegations of Grundyism that have been levelled against her. She
may well be wrong and Mrs Wistrich right but at least it is a
rational and logical point of view she is expressing which ex-
cludes her from the company of some of our contemporary
bigots and demagogues.

Mary Whitehouse had already had her clashes with Enid
Wistrich, until recently chairman of the Greater London Film
Reviewing Board, and recognised her for a formidable opponent.
She had debated against her at Southwark Cathedral and had
continued the argument through the correspondence columns
of newspapers. When in 1974 Mrs Wistrich published her report
which if implemented by the GLC would have meant the abolition of film censorship in the area under their control, Mary at
once secured a copy. 'I immediately realised how much of it was
based on biased reporting and how much the whole thing didn't
stand up from the point of view of *fact*. One of her major platforms—and one which has become part of the gospel of the
anti-censorship lobby—was the findings of the US Presidential
Commission on Obscenity and Pornography, as published in
1969. This report recommended that the obscenity laws in
America should be repealed because "in sum, empirical research
designed to clarify the question has found no evidence to date
that exposure to explicit sexual material plays a significant role

in the causation of delinquent and criminal behaviour among youth and adults''. Today that passage has become the gospel so far as the anti-censorship lobby is concerned but I knew from my links in America that it was a very dubious statement. I also knew that the American Senate had thrown out the Commission's Report because they saw it as a biased piece of propaganda.'

Mary Whitehouse at once swung into action. A call to Professor V. B. Cline, Professor of Psychology at the University of Utah and a dissenting member of the Commission, brought the news that he had just published a book *Where Do You Draw The Line?* which, according to Mrs Whitehouse, 'amounts to an exposé of the strategy of the libertarians on the Commission, who were pre-determined, largely on ideological grounds, to produce a report recommending an end to censorship and that it was because of the subjective nature of the report that the American administration overwhelmingly rejected the Report'. Cline promised to airmail a copy at once.

Another call to Adelaide, Australia, reached Dr John Court whom Mary had met in Australia and who had toured Britain, Denmark, Sweden and Holland in the summer of 1974 to draw up a research report on the pornography scene in Europe. Court's report had just been finished and, in fact, was actually in the process of being typed. Hot off the electric typewriter, he would rush her a copy.

'So I got both these things and sat down one Sunday—I sat down at nine in the morning—I got my housecoat on—and I said to Ernest, "With your support and approval I'm not going to move" I sat down in that chair you're sitting in—"I'm not going to move until I've gone through Mrs Wistrich's report and checked each of her statements." So I sat there until 7.30 without moving—and I just went through it and produced a pamphlet called *Mrs Mary Whitehouse Replies to Mrs Enid Wistrich* and I took it point by point. For instance, on the point of no evidence that exposure to explicit material did harm, I said "did you not know that nearly 90 per cent of the evidence showing harmful effects was omitted from the material presented to the Commission?"'

Mrs Whitehouse's rebuttal constitutes a formidable reply—although it is easy enough to argue that anybody can juggle 'facts' and 'statistics' (but, of course, that also goes for the other side of the argument). Why, she asked, had Mrs Wistrich not looked at the updated (1973) findings of the Presidential Commission which included (1) Five studies linking pornography and sexual arousal with aggression; (2) 254 psychotherapists who found pornography to be an instigator or contributor to a sex crime; (3) that media violence was found to be a model for sado-masochistic and sexually violent behaviour? Did Mrs Wistrich know that some of the statistics relating to Danish and US sex crimes were reported to the Commission in 1969 as exactly the opposite to the original sources?

She belaboured every one of Mrs Wistrich's favourite themes. 'No evidence' of sexual material influencing criminal behaviour was due simply to the fact that 90 per cent of the research showing it did was omitted from the Commission's Report. A study of 476 reformatory inmates had, in fact shown the very opposite. Sex crimes had certainly diminished in Denmark as Mrs Wistrich argued—but this was due to the fact that laws against certain sex offences had been relaxed in the Sixties and therefore acts previously considered criminal were no longer subject to prosecution. In fact, the incidence of rape and attempted rape in Copenhagen had risen significantly since anti-censorship attitudes had been accepted. Nobody raised a cry any longer when they saw a man in a dark alley with a little girl. In the USA, rape had increased by 146 per cent between 1960/71; in Britain, too, the incidence of sex crimes was on the increase. How could 'censorship be the province of the courts' when the law was 'confused and ineffective in this field'. To the view that 'the GLC should not be the agent of enforced morality' —'is it really being the agent of "enforced morality" to say that pornography which deals with, for instance, human excrement, bondage and torture, sex with children and animals (all of which may well be seen on our screens in the near future if the changes for which you are campaigning take place!) has no place in the cinemas of our capital city? Or is it commonsense and basic moral responsibility? To take action which would enable such films to be shown would mean that the GLC had become an agent for enforced immorality'. In conclusion Mrs Whitehouse argued that a removal of censorship, far from being 'progressive' would be 'reactionary' and was likely to result in a greater tolerance of violence and sexual deviancy.

Copies of this broadside were sent to every member of the GLC and also to the press.

The day before the debate, Mary was invited to lunch with Horace Cutler, leader of the Tories on the GLC. She laughs heartily at the recollection. 'It was really rather amusing and typical of the way the BBC handled the whole thing. We were having lunch when the BBC came on and said they wanted somebody to balance Mrs Wistrich on *Nationwide*. But the two councillors they wanted were unavailable and Horace Cutler suggested that no doubt I'd be available. But they wouldn't have that. Thames TV, however, were only too happy to have me on twice.'

She spent the rest of the day at the GLC being introduced to various members including many Labour councillors—'with whom I got on very well'. On the morning of the debate, she attended 'that marvellous demonstration by the Festival of Light'. What bucked her almost more than anything else, however, was the reaction of ordinary members of the public to her efforts. One taximan refused to take her fare insisting that he supported her. A second asked her if she would come and speak at a meeting in the East End: 'It's full of your fans,' he declared.

She had dinner at the GLC on the night of the Great Debate, which was due to start at 9 p.m. Radio London had arranged with her that day to 'have a quick word' with her during the debate. 'I presumed that this was normal practice. What I didn't know was that the GLC had never given permission before for a meeting to be broadcast live.' She took her seat at the front of the public gallery when the debate opened. 'When the debate had been going for half an hour, the Radio London people seated at the other side of a pillar whispered that they'd like a word with me and so they came round and put the earphones on my head. I'd only got four words out of my mouth when up jumped the Labour Chief Whip (Harvey Hinds) and objected in the strongest terms that there "was a member of the public being interviewed on the radio".

'I felt absolutely terrible. There was quite a stir downstairs—everybody was very cross about it. I threw the earphones off my head and wriggled back to my place but, blow me, if London Broadcasting didn't come down the steps to where I was sitting and shove a tape recorder in front of me and ask me what I thought of what had happened. I didn't say a word to them—I was so upset. But the councillor next to Mrs Wistrich jumped up to say there was more commotion in the gallery and at this point, the chairman, Dr David Pitt (now Lord Pitt), rose and announced that if there were any more commotions he would order the public gallery cleared. Then the security people came in and I rather wished the floor could open and swallow me.

'I wouldn't have caused such a commotion for worlds—if I hadn't thought that being interviewed like that was perfectly normal. Anyway, as one of the newspapers put it afterwards, it was like a pantomime—the Two Mrs W's Show.

'Time and again National VALA was referred to ni the debate. One councillor spent the whole of his time attacking us. Who were we? Who was this Mrs Whitehouse—this papier maché figure? Several tore me to shreds—one asked who did I dare to think I was, opposing Mrs Wistrich? Yet others spoke up for me—for us.'

The great tragic-comedy continued until 2.30 a.m.—with elements of farce taking over at times so far as Mrs Whitehouse

was concerned. At one stage the Chamber divided and when
they came back it was announced that they had decided to
accept Mrs Wistrich's report by 50 votes to 44. A crestfallen Mrs
Whitehouse was immediately besieged by reporters and in order
to avoid a repetition of the earlier unseemly commotions, went
outside with them. How did she feel? Was she badly upset?
What would she do now? In the middle of the barrage, another
reporter rushed out to announce loudly that the proceedings
were far from over. The GLC had simply voted to 'receive' Mrs
Wistrich's report—not necessarily to accept it. So far it was a
pure technicality.

'So back we all trooped and a motion was put with an
amendment that censorship should be repealed for twelve
months as an experiment. This was *lost* by exactly the same
number as before—which meant that the libertarians had lost.'
Within minutes, Mrs Whitehouse's triumph was complete when
the defeated Enid announced that she intended to resign. 'There
is absolutely no point in my staying,' she declared angrily.

For Mrs Whitehouse it was huzzahs and excitement all the
way now with the press continually clamouring for her attention. Eventually they allowed her to go to her hotel—but they
invaded her bedroom the next morning even before she was out
of bed, seeking more opinions and quotes.

At mid-day she was at the studios of one of the ITV companies, all set for a personal confrontation with Mrs Wistrich—a
programme which had been arranged before the result of the
vote was known. 'I was waiting in the Green Room (a hospitality
room where people who are to appear on programmes wait)
when Mrs Wistrich came in,' explains Mary Whitehouse.
'Normally, she's a very controlled sort of person. But this time
when she came in, she flung her arms out and said "No doubt,
you're feeling very happy today, Mrs Whitehouse". To which I
replied softly "I'm always happy".'

To everyone's astonishment, Mrs Wistrich resolutely refused
to take part in any discussion with Mary Whitehouse. She

would talk to the chairman but not directly to Mrs Whitehouse. 'In the event, the chairman had to chat to me and then I went out of picture and then he chatted to her.' Later, when they were off the air, Mrs Wistrich remarked, 'At least you and I agree about one thing, Mrs Whitehouse—we both think that there should be a change in the law.' Mrs Whitehouse had announced on the programme that she and a deputation intended to see the Home Secretary with a view to having the law on films changed. 'She even said she was prepared to sign a joint letter with me to the Home Secretary requesting a change in the law,' says Mary, quickly adding, 'But I was fairly sure that the changes she wanted and the changes I wanted were not the same. What she wanted—and still wants—I'm convinced, is a law which takes away the right of local authorities to license films for viewing in their own areas. But National VALA and I are concerned to keep the power in the hands of local authorities because it's the only way grassroots opinion can make its voice heard.'

When Mrs Whitehouse buckles on her armour to do battle, she has little doubt but that she is acting as the champion of grassroots opinion. To her the Enid Wistrichs of this world are the elitist 'experts' who are responsible to no one and whose expressed opinions are so far removed from the normal experience of the vast majority of people in Britain that their views amount to an almost complete distortion of the national will.

It is a concept, of course which it is not possible either to sustain or disprove. On the whole, Mary Whitehouse, while recognising that a large proportion of the English nation no longer professes any formal religious belief, remains convinced that it still accepts those moral precepts first handed down on Mount Sinai and which, refined and enlarged throughout more than three millenia, provide the structure of parliamentary democracy.

CHAPTER THIRTEEN

Mary Whitehouse Today

Mary Whitehouse is now just a half a decade away from the biblical three score and ten. I can detect no signs of smugness nor self-satisfaction about her. She seems to be blissfully unaware of her own niche in British national life; uninterested in personal fame and identity—save only in so far as they serve the Cause. If people know of her and accept her as a spokesman, then she is happy to be part of the armoury of the Lord. One thing that has to be said about her is that, unlike the vast majority of her countrymen and women, she is neither apathetic, confused nor disillusioned. In common with Communists (or Marx-aligned groups) she has a clear-cut philosophy and knows exactly where she wants to go. On the whole, one senses, it would be unfair to label her as standing four-square for the *status quo*. Her own life and the bedrock of her beliefs rest on the assumption that all human life and activity is transitory. She is not a historian; but she has a deep sense of what once happened in Judaea and the hills of Galilee. She is sensitive to evolutionary as well as revolutionary processes and can see them at work within her own life.

During long sessions of questioning Mrs Whitehouse, one observes several little traits. The way questions and the need to supply answers, to debate and discuss, rouses her from her temporarily exhausted torpor and leaves her sparkling and happy. One notes the pauses and hesitations occasionally as she weighs a question and wonders if there is anything there to hide —and then realises, in evaluating her answer, that all that is involved is the need for a woman getting on in age for time to marshal her answers, to not commit herself to a haphazard thought, to remember that her words are weighed by her enemies. She is capable of the sharp Churchillian note as when she crisply guillotined my rather unrighteous attempt to re-open the question of her youthful romance with a married man. That was a private world and a private affair that had nothing to do with anybody else. She would only underline the fact that, unlike the consequences of such an emotional involvement today, there was no carnal knowledge involved.

It is easy to question the basis of her support—apart altogether from her personal philosophy. Does a membership of 31,000 people really permit her a national voice on the scale which she has now achieved? And yet as the commentator Francis Boyd has pointed out in the *Guardian*, 'the dedicated Communist would reply: "There are more Communists in the world than members of any other parties". This may not be true, since party membership is notoriously small anywhere'—and indeed, one has only to reflect on the insignificant number of Communist party members within the Soviet Union itself to realise how unreliable a guide this sort of reasoning is.

There is the background of those 'suspect' affiliations—the Oxford Group and Moral Rearmament. She talks freely—certainly as freely as I, who know little of either movement, can make her. She runs swiftly over the history of the Oxford Group, the small band of Oxford students who believed that if you gave yourself to God, he would guide you; who accepted the four moral absolutes—absolute honesty, absolute purity, absolute unselfishness, absolute love; who got their name because a stationmaster stuck a label *Oxford Group* on some reserved carriages in a railway train—and that name seemed as good as any.

She is not evasive about Moral Rearmament. The war changed everything, she says. The Oxford Group had faded away, but then Frank Buchman came to England and talked about the need for the moral rearmament of the British nation. She attended some of their meetings; went to the plays and

musicals they staged. Of course, the movement was conscious of
Communist infiltration—in the immediate post-war years,
wasn't everybody? Hadn't the Russian armies seized half of the
most ancient and civilised parts of Europe? Hadn't they turned
that most Catholic of countries, Poland, into a Communist state;
tossed young King Michael of Roumania off his throne; over-
thrown the great parliamentary democracy of Czechoslovakia,
divided Germany, the heartland, into two? Hadn't the Communist brought the very epicentre of Western civilisation, magnificent France itself, to prostration? Wasn't it only the American atomic bomb which prevented the Red Army marching to
the Bay of Biscay?

'But in so many other ways, it was a non-political movement,'
she insists. 'It was not against Conservatism, against Labour,
against Liberal. It was ecumenical before that became the
fashionable and accepted thing. Even in its opposition to Communism, it was not trying to fight a political ideal; it didn't even
see Communism as the main enemy. As the Christian has always
looked at the problem, it saw sin as the enemy—and philo-
sophies such as Communism based on materialism obviously
fostered sin because any preoccupation with materialism must
turn people into selfish beings. MRA said what I think is still
true—that until you change men themselves, you can never
change society. Society is only a reflection of what individuals
feel and think—and I don't believe you can change society
without changing men; if you try to do so, then you only land
yourself with a dictatorship, either of the Right or Left. So that
as I see it, the difference is whether society allows itself to be
manipulated by men—or guided by God. The belief that God
can guide has never left me. Neither have I ever gone back on
my basic decision to give my life to God. The basic commitment
has remained.'

When she married and was looking after her children, her
association with such movements as the Oxford Group and
MRA waned. 'I had that much less time for meetings and so on.

I don't go to MRA meetings any more but I still have friends in the movement. Certainly, I never formally resigned, so to speak. If anything'—here she laughs that hearty hockey-field laugh—'it was the other way round—MRA resigned from me! At first, indeed, I think they would have liked to have had a greater influence on us, to have been behind first the Clean-Up TV campaign and later National VALA. But from the beginning I was determined that this thing of ours had to be a completely independent organisation and I've kept it that way. Today I can truthfully say that MRA has no controlling influence or position in National VALA nor is there any question of its people being involved *per se*.

'I will admit this, of course—but it has to be understood properly—that it is probably true to say, in one sense anyway, that you can never stop being a member of MRA. But that is simply because membership means that your life is changed for you—by God—and that that change in your life must remain.'

Her world is now a vastly different one from those days when she travelled the Midlands with the eager young band of Oxford students who believed that they had rediscovered the secrets of the first-century Christians. Now her life is an often frenetic one of TV appearances, debates, discussions, press conferences, cheering crowds, world tours, phone calls out and into and from every quarter of the English-speaking world.

There came a letter from Sir Michael Swann, chairman of the BBC. VALA's annual convention had passed a resolution calling upon the BBC to do something about bad language on programmes which they, the IBA and even the Annan Committee (now inquiring into broadcasting) admitted aroused the largest volume of complaints; she had passed the resolution on to Sir Michael and now his reply lay on her desk. Where, he demanded in effect, had she ever dug up such an idea; it wasn't true. 'Isn't true,' she hoots triumphantly and showed me page 24 of the BBC's official Handbook Report. Poor Sir Michael—he had indubitably been caught napping. She showed me the words for myself and they unquestionably did read: 'The commonest cause of complaint remains the use of bad language.'

Capably and efficiently, she deals with the distortions and innuendoes which either by malice or incompetence have mis-represented her attitudes in public. 'They say I was against the miners during the miners' strike. What absolute nonsense—quite false. What VALA objected to was one particular pro-gramme where the *balance* of the programme was heavily in favour of the miners. What we were concerned about was the *lack of balance*, not the merits or demerits of the miners' case.

Abortion?—no, she wasn't against medical abortion, nor the legalisation of it. What she was concerned about was the *lack of balance*, the hysteria, that had swept television, both in docu-mentary programmes or in plays so that all the other issues involved in the subject were blanketed out. Would legalisation lead to abortion on demand? dubious clinics? abortion as a form of birth control? 'All these issues were simply swept aside.'

She worries about the way radio and TV 'promote' ideas, turning matters in which most people are totally uninterested into burning topics of the day. What kind of ideas?

'Take euthanasia, for instance. I can't believe that euthanasia is really a burning topic with the people of this country—yet we in VALA have noticed that over the past six months radio and TV have been doing their best to turn it into an issue. There was one extremely well done programme on the subject—a Dutch programme about the trial of a woman doctor who had killed her mother. I thought that very well done—very well-balanced; then right at the end, somebody in London pops up with con-cluding remarks which weighted the whole programme in favour of euthanasia. That was followed by Beverley Nichols talking on radio about his personal plight. Then there were letters support-ing his views. Suddenly euthanasia had been elevated into a public, if not a burning issue. One really has to ask whether there are people inside the BBC who have a vested interest in some way in euthanasia.'

It is not, in many ways, an altogether enviable life to lead. There are the frustrations; the constant need to watch and note; to avoid making a fool of oneself; to ground one's argument on reasonable premises. She is aware that people have seen her straining, seemingly, at gnats.

And yet, as her campaign continues, heavy guns are heard barking along the same lines she has been promulgating for years. Sir Michael Swann, talking at a Leeds University seminar in March 1975, talks about 'a bias against understanding' in TV and radio and relates this to the 'conventional values of TV news and current affairs'. He suggests that in concentrating solely on a situation, the coverage neglects issues. Programmes showed what was wrong but did not widen the context sufficiently to show how things went wrong or what might be done to put them right. 'For the broadcasters to expose the ills of society without exposing the difficulty of curing them and the need for quiet determination and patience on the part of reformers is only to reinforce the naïvety of activities of every political shade.' Mary Whitehouse almost visibly preens herself —if the phrase is allowable about a woman who seems to have successfully subordinated excesses of the ego: 'This makes me feel how many of the basic tenets of our views are now being accepted.'

Yet she remains aware that a vast body of these television ills that Sir Michael refers to are not the result of incompetence, short-sightedness or ordinary human fallibility. Too, too many of these ill-put-together programmes are deliberately so devised —are the TV equivalents of such blanket left-wing slogans as the chant 'Heath Out, Heath Out'. 'We see it in all sorts of issues—on the question of South Africa, for instance. There is never any assessment of the historic development that has led to this—of how and where the changes would need to come. As a body, we are careful not to come down on one side or the other in these issues. But what we insist is that the public at large is being constantly denied the right to form a proper judgment on dozens of issues.' In other words, it is being fed the slogan and not the debate. She goes on: 'What we've got to do is to train a generation to be able to listen to a programme and to be able to understand it, to decide for themselves whether the makers are prejudiced or biased or whether they have made an honest and objective attempt to tell the truth. The new generation has to be educated to TV, to be able to interpret and read it properly. We've got—all of us—to stand up and ask: Is the BBC, is television, our master or our servant? Is it manipulating us—and if it is, how long are we going to permit it to do so?'

Some of it is fun. Off to Claridges to address the Thirty Club— Lord Cudlipp, Lord Ryder, John Freeman, Lord Birkett and so on. Fun and games on a David Frost phone-in programme with the extraordinary Arthur Scargill who whiled away the time in the Green Room before the programme saying that he had more power than any MP; relating how certain Labour MPs met with him 'regularly' to hear his views. The night of the great debate before the Cambridge University Union when the crowd suddenly burst into laughter at one of her remarks and when she demanded to know 'What's so funny about that?' turned to find that a student had dangled a skull down behind her and somebody had observed, 'Alas, poor Mugg.' The attempt to shock her at Manchester University's College of Science and Technology by 'streakers'; 'The platform was all lit up—and the rest of the auditorium in blackness. At one moment, I happened to glance down at the papers on my knee—and at that very moment, apparently someone "streaked". When I looked up, I was aware of a kind of commotion in the top corner of the room but I saw nothing. When somebody shouted out, "What did you think of that happening?" I could only reply honestly, "What happening? I didn't see any happening." If I'd waited a second longer before looking down at my papers,

I'd have seen the fellow, of course. Remarkable, really.'

There was also memories of Leicester, where the students had behaved like animals, of other campuses where the New Left had filled the halls with their supporters and where strategic lines of retreat had to be organised for her.

But, suddenly, it has all begun to change. A new spirit is sweeping the campuses; the younger generation is, seemingly, ready again to listen to an opinion other than its own. At Manchester, a red-haired student stands up and declares, 'Mrs Whitehouse, I came here for a good giggle—but I want to apologise—and I'm not alone in that, I'm sure. Instead, I find myself in almost total agreement with everything you say.'

The days of stormy passages may well be over. 'My public image works to my advantage, of course,' she admits. 'It brings in the crowds. And then, in the second place, they all seem so dumbstruck by the level on which I start to talk—and so I'm away!'

Mary Whitehouse now speaks in a much more formidable style—normally off the cuff. 'If I have to debate—I'm not a debater—I have to prepare what I'm going to say very carefully. If I have to make a speech, then on the way I just jot down a few notes to give myself a feeling of security—but in fact, I speak out extemporaneously.'

Once, she restricted her speeches to the condemnation and belabouring of the BBC or specific TV programmes. Now she has changed her tone and her tack—and as such, has converted herself into a figure that can never again be easily laughed at or dismissed unthinkingly.

'Now, I range over the whole historical and philosophical issues raised by the work we do. Once I spoke on a very day-to-day basis but now I know that my biggest job is not to persuade people to agree with me—even to see a particular programme as I do—because I now believe that this has become an irrelevance. What matters is what other people feel—and I want them to make *their* voices heard. I emphasise this the whole way along.

I emphasise that if they understand the philosophy of things, then they can make up their own minds—not have it manipulated for them.

'We in VALA have now gathered so many facts and information from all over the world that I feel my function is to offer students and others ideas and facts so that they can decide themselves, discuss for themselves. I see my function as filling in the empty spaces in the current debate around such issues as the permissive society and censorship. The issue of censorship is basic to our whole work, my whole work. Censorship has become a very emotive word—almost the dirtiest word in the English language. I try to give my listeners the information and background that will allow them to understand that the idea that we are facing a choice between the seventies and Victorianism is totally false. I try to point out that after the First World War we were developing steadily and naturally and at an even pace a much more open and liberal approach to such ideas as sex and sexual behaviour, but at a pace society could assimilate. And then I point out that in the late fifties, certain forces moved into the scene. I identify these forces—right across the board. Financial interest—the professional pornographers. The humanist attack. I point out that what we're getting is not an increasingly free society, but an increasingly conformist society.

'I open up the political attacks on our structures. I quote from James Michener's book *What Happened at Kent State—and Why* where he says that numerous committed revolutionaries have preached that the debasement of language is essential to the destruction of society. I go on to say that I want my listeners to understand that when I speak out against the use of four-letter words on TV, I'm not only concerned with crudities of speech or offences against taste but the fact is that, as any teacher will know, four-letter words are essentially part of adolescent culture; a way boys have of expressing their burgeoning sexuality, which is usually done in a crude and aggressive fashion. That up until this point in time, the whole weight of our culture has been to help our young—to teach them to leave that stage behind and to go on to more beautiful and delicate ways of expressing themselves and living, but that what has now happened is that instead of the establishment trying to help the young, the establishment itself is going back and joining the adolescent culture and the results are that the new generations are being cut off from their cultural history. I outline the political pressures, the social pressures, the apathy of the British people, which means that we are raising children who are completely vulnerable. I point out that the British people have had all their sureties and securities undermined or torn away from them—that they are now uncertain where they are not apathetic.

'And finally, I talk about the myths of censorship. The myth that nobody is affected by what they see or read. It is a measure of the irrationality that is gripping Britain that we can all sit there with solemn faces and listen to people deny that sublime communication cannot elevate and that degraded communication cannot degrade. I ask what is education but knowledge based on the written word? I state that the whole attack is like Hitler's lie. I ask them to pause and consider if, just for a moment, they would deny that the world has been changed by the Bible, *Mein Kampf* or *Das Kapital*.'

The laughing, she feels, has finally stopped.

It has certainly stopped so far as the British government is concerned. Mrs Whitehouse and National VALA have played a not insignificant part in the movement to prevent the public display of indecent or titillating material—on billboards, in underground stations, on bookstalls and elsewhere.

For some time she and her executive committee had been concerned by the fact that the public can avoid less and less easily this material. In her concern for public decency, it is fair to say that Mrs Whitehouse was not ploughing a new furrow. As the law stands, anybody attempting to bathe naked in the fountains in Trafalgar Square is certain to end up before the beak. On the whole, British society would still consider it offensive if people walked about without clothes on in public or had sexual intercourse in full daylight in the shadow of Eros. The objection to displays of nudity or sexual intercourse by photographic or other representation, therefore, clearly betokens no departure in principle.

Mrs Whitehouse herself—at her age and after all she has had to wallow through during her self-inflicted duties—would admit that there is very little that could be displayed on a billboard that would shock her. But, of course, she is concerned solely with principle—the liberty of the individual not to have his sensibilities assaulted without his consent. It is one thing for a man— or a woman—to buy a ticket for a blue-movie in a private club; to buy a 'girlie' or 'boyie' magazine; to read a 'dirty' book. It might be argued that everybody would be better off if such things were not available—but it is equally valid to argue that a man or woman has a right to make a choice. There, at any rate, lies room for debate and discussion.

Mary would not allow, however, that the right to pursue pornography—if there is any such right—should be extended to permit pornography to pursue the individual. The flaunting of sex, violence, sado-masochistic practices and so on in a public place where a child or an adolescent—or even just an ordinary adult who wants to retain the privacy of his thoughts—is something she believes should be fought.

Pornographic display had already been discussed within her organisation but nothing had been done until the day when the Appeal judges overturned the sentences in the Oz trial in 1971. When the newspaper reporters overwhelmed her for comment, Mary Whitehouse felt that the time for action had arrived. With the aid of *Festival of Light* supporters, a nationwide petition was organised. It was a massive job, lasting over twelve months—the biggest petition organised in Britain for more than sixty years. All over the country volunteers tramped from door to door, asking for signatures to a petition which demanded a reform of the present obscenity laws; the extension of the law to radio and television; a proper control of how sex education was presented in schools. The 'spread' of approach was as wide as possible without the aid of a computer. The attempt was an honest one to ascertain the feelings of a genuine cross-section of the nation. Semi-detacheds, flats, council-houses, estates, bungalows, caravans, detached homes, high-rise blocks—people living in every kind of residence—were approached. The lowest percentage of response was 69%, the highest 95%, giving an overall figure in favour of 85%. Mary Whitehouse insists—and it would not be easy to deny her assertion—that this represents grass-roots opinion. Over one and a half million signatures were obtained which, however one considers it, represents a formidable group.

In the wake of the petition, Mrs Whitehouse was received by Mr Heath, then Prime Minister; at the Home Office; and had talks with Sir John Eden, then Minister of Communications. She is sure that it was in response to this massive petition plus Lord Longford's Report on Pornography (she lays stress on the importance of the Longford Report as a factor) that the Conservative Party decided to introduce an Indecent Displays Act. This Bill would have gone a long way towards satisfying her demands. Oddly enough, on the technicality that radio and television are not public displays (they are beamed into private homes), they could not be included in the Bill but Sir John Eden assured Mary that the BBC and IBA chiefs had indicated that they would work within 'the spirit' of the act. Out went the Tories, however, and the new Labour Government did not pursue the Bill. The press made some fuss about Mrs Whitehouse's attitude—and for a while she risked being labelled as anti-Labour. But she explains, 'It's got nothing to do with whether I'm anti-Labour or not. We're not a political party—we're not supporting Tories or Labour; all we're out to do is to support whatever party produces a bill we consider satisfactory. Our stand—my stand—is that we support the Bill—and it doesn't matter to us which party introduces it. We're not in the business of party politics in any fashion.'

Though the Bill has been dropped, the question of indecent public displays has not. The matter has been kept under Government review (in the Home Office) and to Mary Whitehouse's delight Shirley Summerskill, junior Minister at the Home Office, sent her a copy of a Government Green Paper on the subject in early April 1975, asking for her comments and recommendations.

'I can only say that I'm absolutely delighted,' declared Mary. 'If these proposals are ever adopted, they would be even better than anything envisaged by the Tory Indecent Displays Bill.'

She never believed she was on her own. Now, she feels, all the ridicule, laughter, abuse, threats—the whole paraphernalia of attack on those who refuse to be bullied into anything or everything—has proved worthwhile. At long last, she is being vindicated; shown not just as a crank but as the spokeswoman for a sincerely held view, widely shared by her countrymen and women.

Following her rough passage at Leicester University—which Mary still regards as one of the most traumatic experiences of her career—she returned home in a state of total exhaustion and was so ill for several days afterwards that she had to take a complete rest. She regards Leicester as a turning point—the Stalingrad and El Alamein of her campaign; thereafter the high tide of Marxist student opposition began to ebb as more moderate people, while not necessarily subscribing to her views, tended towards the opinion that she was being unjustifiably villified and abused.

In her own mind, it was the prelude to something even more important; a happening which she sees in an almost mystical light. While she was ill, Malcolm Muggeridge telephoned to ask how she was. When she told him, he expressed outrage and anger and then, almost in despair, asked, 'Mary, what are we going to do for these young people?' As they talked, they felt

'Why don't we have some great demonstration? Why don't we have a Festival of Light?' Thus the idea, which was not destined to reach fruition for another two years, was born.

Not that she and Malcolm Muggeridge did not try to bring it about sooner. 'It was our vision—but I was not destined to carry it out; I was not meant to organise it, that task was left to other hands.' On and off, between 1969 when she was so abused by the students of Leicester University and April 1971 when the great gathering known as The Festival of Light took place in Trafalgar Square, she and Muggeridge made several abortive attempts to stage the Festival at the Albert Hall. 'It was very curious' she says, 'but something always got in the way—either the hall wasn't available or the pressure of other events stopped Malcolm and I staging the affair.'

The idea, indeed, lay dormant until a young missionary called Peter Hill returned from India and more or less came to the realisation that he had been labouring in the wrong country. He had left a Britain still ostensibly possessed of the Roman virtues; still ostensibly a Christian country and professing a Christian culture. He returned to find it sunk in greed and sloth—its values under continual assault by the forces of decadence and political subversion. He spent five days in retreat, praying—in the course of which, according to Mary, he had a vision; a gathering of thousands of young people in Trafalgar Square declaring their rejection of the New Morality which vested interests were trying to force upon them. Determined to bring such a gathering about but at a loss how to achieve it, he consulted the Reverend Edward Stride who happened to be a London friend of Mary Whitehouse. Stride suggested he meet Mary. Hill and his wife visited Mary and she told him about the efforts she and Malcolm Muggeridge had made to stage a Festival of Light and what their idea was. She then put the young missionary in touch with Malcolm Muggeridge and thus was born the Festival of Light.